THE HAUNTINGS OF TWO SISTERS

SHOCKING TRUE-LIFE EXPERIENCES

Pam Mandel with Karen Pena

Printed in the United States of America

Print ISBN: 978-1735104706
E-Book ISBN: 978-1735104713

Canoe Tree
Press

4697 Main Street
Manchester Center, VT 05255

Canoe Tree Press is a division of DartFrog Books.

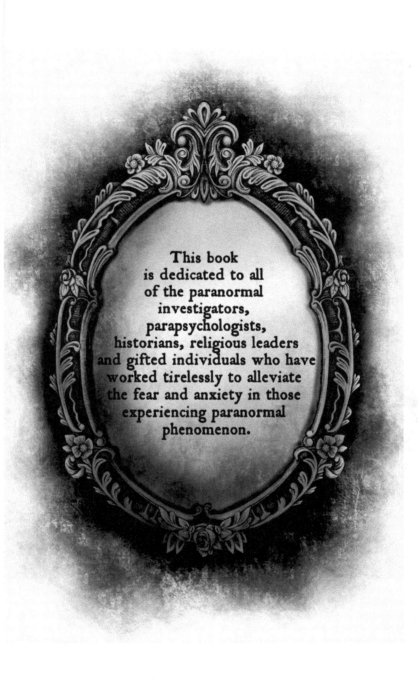

This book
is dedicated to all
of the paranormal
investigators,
parapsychologists,
historians, religious leaders
and gifted individuals who have
worked tirelessly to alleviate
the fear and anxiety in those
experiencing paranormal
phenomenon.

Pam and Karen with our parents in 1969

OUR STORIES

FOREWORD

What do you do when you see dead people and you're married to a minister? Pam believed you keep your mouth shut! And that is exactly what she did for over fifteen years. Well, that was until their divorce. Her sister Karen's emotional journey from losing her baby after nine years of trying to conceive created the perfect storm for them to go on a paranormal roller coaster ride that had numerous highs, lows, sharp turns, and even a few 360s along the way.

With one of the most controversial topics that stirs up so much passion from both the believer and non-believer, these two sisters, two years apart and in their mid-sixties, finally came to the point in their lives where they felt comfortable sharing publicly their gifts and paranormal experiences.

If you have ever seen a ghost or heard a spirit, you may recognize some of the similarities in the true stories they are recounting in their book. We believe the realms that we live in are governed by spiritual laws. And those dimensions are inhabited by beings who observe us, interact with us, manipulate us, and most frightening, at times seek our destruction. For every demon who comes to terrify, deceive and manipulate, there are angels who work to protect God's beloved children from the forces of evil.

There are certain mysteries that are kept from human understanding that we don't pretend to know. Pam and Karen are hoping that by reading their book, it gives you more awareness of the world that we all live in. Certainly not in a way that makes you paranoid or afraid that demons are going to pop out of the corner of your living room. But in a way that will help you with discernment. Perhaps you yourself were a child who went to your parents telling them that someone was in your closet, only to be ignored and left alone in the dark. Perhaps your child has knocked on your door at some point, wide-eyed because there was someone in your house that they knew didn't belong, but you dismissed it as childish imagination.

But then there is experience, cold, hard experience. For those of us who are open to the possibility of the existence of realms beyond those of the senses and intellect, you see something that others don't. You sense that there very well may be worlds out there that are waiting to intersect our well-traveled and familiar daily paths.

Their stories cover personal paranormal experiences from premonitions, demonic attacks, angels, and ghosts' dogs, to visits from loved ones. Join them in their crazy carnival ride while you read the following accounts of interactions that two sisters, their loved ones, and their friends have had with those dimensions. Read their journey in which their lives have been changed and redirected by these unique encounters.

TYPES OF HAUNTINGS

Within our book we share experiences of four types of hauntings: Intelligent Haunting, Residual Haunting, Poltergeist Haunting, and, most terrifying, Demonic Haunting. Below is a brief description of each.

Intelligent Hauntings: Intelligent Hauntings are when the ghosts can have eye contact and might try to communicate or interact with the living. Maybe the ghost is not aware that he or she has died, or they just want to stay around their loved ones. We feel our Mom and her interactions with us is a good example of this.

Residual Hauntings: Residual Hauntings are usually hauntings that keep repeating themselves. Maybe you will hear footsteps in an empty room or dishes being done at the same time every day. The ghosts that fall into this category hardly ever interact with the living and are relatively harmless. We think at times this is the category that our animals fall into.

Poltergeist Hauntings: Poltergeist Hauntings are noisy ghosts who sometimes make loud noises by running upstairs, slamming doors, throwing objects, or even carrying out physical attacks. They will often move an object from one location to another, causing you to think you are losing your mind.

Demonic Hauntings: In Demonic Hauntings, the demon's main goal is to destroy any good in your home. It will take advantage of your sorrow and cause deep depression. In one of our chapters, all laughter left our home and the tension grew stronger and stronger. As we describe in some of our chapters, it would start off as a shadow out of the corner of your eye, then a darker-than-dark shadow man, black grasshoppers, and even a hell hound. What we have experienced is the more fear you show, the stronger they become with the potential finale being actual demonic attacks.

I Told You So!

Pam Mandel

1962 - 1969

I n 1962, when I was six and my sister Karen was four, we moved from Daly City, just south of San Francisco, across the Bay to a town called Fremont. It was typical small-town America, a place where you knew all your neighbors and never locked your doors. It was still a beautiful area at the time, dotted with orchards and open spaces. It was a place where neighborhood kids rode their bikes to their heart's content, and no one thought twice about hitting her neighbor up for a cup of sugar or those two eggs that were needed for her recipe. Whatever crime existed was almost negligible, petty stuff like kids throwing fruit at a house or chasing a cat up a tree.

Ironically enough, it was during this happy time and in this happy setting that something not quite as idyllic entered my life. You see, it was then that I started to have premonitions, good and bad. Similar instances persisted throughout my childhood, and I was no stranger to the feeling of something gnawing at me way down deep. Despite the efforts of more than a few people to saddle me with labels, I have always hesitated to use them. What is undeniable are the warnings I´ve received in my life from some protective entity on the other side—maybe God or a loved one—when something negative was about to happen. For example, once when my family was en route to Disneyland, I had a sudden premonition that we were going to get a flat tire. It was only a few minutes after my father had dismissed my warning with a great big grin that we felt the car driving funny. I told you so: flat tire!

However, the most extreme situation took place when I was in my early teens and involved a run-in with a prowler in our neighborhood.

One blistering summer night in 1969, with the temperature reaching into the 100s, Dad went night fishing with our next-door neighbor. It was a two-hour drive up to their favorite fishing spot on Frank's Tract, located in the California Delta. They were not a hop, skip, and a jump from home (a fact that had a great bearing on what was about to happen). In those days, almost no one had air conditioning, so in our homes all doors and windows were wide open. At this time, I was a brand-new teenager at age thirteen. And Karen was eleven.

There was an extremely weird vibe in the air that night, and it made me very restless and anxious. It was just too strong to be ignored. I had this feeling that something really bad was going to happen, and I knew exactly what it was. At about 6:30 p.m. I went into the kitchen, where Mom was cleaning up after dinner. When I shared my premonition, she looked at me with her eyes wide opened—her patented "Oh no, what is this daughter of mine going to lay on me now?" look—and asked me what on earth I was talking about. I told her that I knew someone was going to break into our house—or worse—and literally begged her to lock everything up like a fortress while there was still time to do so.

Unfortunately, she wasn't buying it.

In fact, she looked at me like I was completely cuckoo and, after verbally branding me with a great big capital "R" for ridiculous, called to my attention the well-known fact that incidents of that nature never, ever happen in Fremont. After she flat out refused to lock any doors or windows, I rushed back to my room, terrified and upset at her refusal to take anything I'd said seriously.

My battle for self-control lost, I re-emerged from my room to deliver the same warning to her. The later it became, the more I panicked because the dread that I felt was so strong, so persistent, that there was no room for doubt. I just knew someone was going to break into our house.

Again, Mom flat out refused to take me seriously.

As the hands on the clock approached 8:30 p.m. and darkness began to fall, I finally crossed over into full-blown panic mode, knowing beyond a shadow of a doubt that someone was about to try to break into our house. By 9:00 p.m., that panic was in full runaway mode, with my fear screaming itself out of me in between bouts of hysterical sobbing. I kept on begging my Mom to shut and lock all the doors and windows because the event of a stranger breaking into our house was getting closer and closer. Once again, she wasn't having it, becoming so upset with me that she sent me to my room.

Now 9:30 p.m. rolled around. Our phone rang. It was our next-door neighbor, the one whose husband is out fishing with Dad. As soon as I heard the phone ring, I knew this was it! All my hysterics, sobbing, and begging the entire evening had all led up to this moment. I came running to the kitchen. Our neighbor was shouting so loudly that Mom had to hold the phone away from her ear, allowing me to hear the conversation. She asked my mom if she was playing a trick on her, to which Mom replied, "No, why?" She said that someone was trying to force her patio door open. Suddenly, my mom ordered me in a voice that was fast losing its composure to hurry and close the patio door tight and lock it!

That was the straw that broke the camel's back. I ran down the hall to the bathroom screaming, "I told you so, I told you so," continuing to scream even after I had locked myself in and jumped in the bathtub for safety. By that time the prowler had jumped the fence into our yard. Mom dropped the phone and ran to the sliding glass patio door, where she found herself standing face to face with him, fighting to close the patio door. After locking the door in his face, she ran to the side window, which was still open. As she closed and locked it, she turned her head just in time to see the prowler leap over the back fence.

Meanwhile, the neighbor had had the presence of mind to call the police, and within minutes they were circling the block with their floodlights looking in between houses and such. Doing a door-to-door search, they eventually caught the prowler in the act of raping a babysitter about three houses behind us. After it was all over, my mom did not want to address how I knew it was going to happen.

I kept repeating, "I told you so, I told you so!"

By now we were all hysterical. My mom called the man across the street and asked him for some help and support. He arrived within minutes, and our next-door neighbor came over with her kids so we could all be hysterical together.

Little did we know at the time, but when all this was happening, our dad was in the fight of his life! Dad was enjoying the heck out of some late-night fishing when suddenly he felt extreme pain below his chest. Doubled over in agony, he did his best to hold on while our neighbor tried to maneuver the boat back to shore; however, a huge windstorm had come up. Great big black waves rocked the boat as he struggled to get to the dock, worried the entire time that the boat might actually capsize. Finally, back on land, he rushed my dad into the car, and they raced back to Fremont. My mom frantically took my dad to the hospital where he was immediately diagnosed with an erupted gallbladder.

The police later told us that the prowler had been scouting our neighborhood for over a week. When I thought about the timing of it all, I could not avoid concluding that we were dealing with a very, very dangerous psychopath. Anyone else would have taken off speedily the moment he was discovered instead of carrying out the thoroughly heinous action he performed with the babysitter. As horrific as the experience was especially for the babysitter, with his past history it could have ended up much worse. When I think back on the events of that night, it's clear to me that God was protecting us all.

Pam and Karen with our Dad in 1959

*Pam and Karen with our Parents
and Grandparents in 1959*

Pam with her Parents in 1957

...But Let's Go
Back in Time

✝

Pam Mandel
1959 - 1969

. . . But let's go back in time.

My dad woke up with the feeling someone was watching him. It was me standing beside his bed staring intently at him.

"What is it, Pam?" Dad asked.

"Popeye is in my room," I said.

This was not the first time we'd had this conversation.

By now we both knew the drill. Dad would get up, take my hand, and walk me down the hallway into my bedroom. He would look under the bed and into the closet. Then he would look in the little corner behind the bedroom door, anywhere anyone could hide. He knew the drill because he had been doing this since I was three years old. My dad would say, "There's no one in the room, Pam, go back to bed." I would crawl back into my bed, and he would tuck me back in followed by a kiss on my cheek. We had done this so many times before. Lying there quietly, I would hear the sound of his footsteps going down the hall back into his bedroom. Now I was alone in the dark.

An hour later, Dad would wake up to find me standing by his bed again.

"What's up?" he would say.

"Popeye is back," I would reply.

The look he would give me was full of love and understanding. He would pick me up and snuggle me into the warmth of his bed right between him and mom. My dad worked hard, and these continued midnight visits by his four-year-old daughter were taking their toll on both of us.

"'Popeye is back,' I said…"

The ghost that would come into my room at night most often in those early years was some spirit I referred to as Popeye. He was an older man, probably in his seventies, always wearing the same outfit. It was one of those stiff white t-shirts from the '50s. His arm muscles were huge, and he had a short black and gray beard. Popeye would always come out of the closet, stand next to my bed, and just stare at me. He never spoke. I called him "Popeye" because he reminded me of the sailor from the old cartoon. I wasn't afraid of him, but it was uncomfortable having a stranger in my room night after night.

Once when I was sitting in front of the television watching the cartoon Popeye, I excitedly pointed at him and looked at my grandma. "I know him!" I said to her. He comes into my room every night!" Grandma just smiled at me.

On other occasions, two middle-aged female ghosts would come into my room. They were close in age and actually reminded me of sisters. They loved to stand at the foot of my bed excitingly talking to each other while staring at me, wildly gesturing at each other with their arms. They spoke so fast that I could never really understand what they were saying. I sensed that they were not there to harm me, so I was not afraid.

Finally, when I was six years old, we moved to a brand new house in Fremont, California. I was excited since I felt we were moving far enough away from all my nighttime visitors. After being in our new house for only a short time, though, things began to start anew.

Karen and Pam Celebrating their Birthdays in November 1960

Karen and Pam Helping our Grandpa with the Chores in 1960

Our parents had no idea what was going on in their houses. But I soon realized that my little sister Karen knew. Sometimes she could see them, too.

At night, Karen would be lying in bed, ready for sleep, when suddenly she would see passing spirits in the hallway walking towards my room. She would quickly hide her face in her pillow, hoping with all her might for them to go away. Occasionally, the spirits would detour into her room, only to stand by her bed staring intently at her. She was only five and more terrified of them than I was. At times, she was so petrified she would jump up dashing through the spirits into my room snuggling into bed next to me. In the morning when I awakened, seeing her next to me, I knew exactly what had occurred.

Once when I was eight or nine, Karen and I were playing outside, when suddenly I noticed a family standing across the street. What caught my eye was the odd way they were dressed.

"Do you see them I asked?"

Karen looked in the direction I was pointing, with her eyes open wide. "Who?"

"The funny dressed family across the street."

Karen shook her head no. "What do they look like?"

It was a family of four. They were all just standing there fixated on us. The father wore a dark floppy-rim hat, and the mother wore a blue and white bonnet with a big bow tied under her chin. The two children, a girl and a boy, were our age. The girl's brown hair was in braids and the boy had on black suspenders. As I looked at them, they faded away right before my eyes!

It was as if my sister and I were trapped together in a world that no one else knew existed, where we could sometimes see and feel the beings that no one else could see but were all around us, everywhere. Even when we could not see them, frequently we could feel that they were there through a chill. We were most aware in the stillness and quiet of the night. We didn't realize it at the time, but we had a gift that had been in our family for generations. It wasn't until years later that we realized that not everybody was able to see supernatural beings.

Eventually, our mom started catching on to the fact that there was something up with her two girls.

In our early childhood, our family went to a neighborhood church. Back then, you simply went to church because it was the social thing to do. Like a lot of families, our mom was raised Christian, but our dad came from a Jewish background.

Despite the difference in religions, we always celebrated Christmas in a huge way. When I was seven years old, our maternal grandparents came over to our house to celebrate the holiday with us. This was always a very special time for Karen and me. The night of Christmas Eve, we followed our tradition of setting out cookies and milk for Santa. The night was even more special because Karen and I got to sleep on the pullout bed in the family room, right next to the cookies and milk, hoping to get a glimpse of Santa.

Suddenly, in the wee hours of the morning, I awoke. I had that creepy, strange feeling that I was being watched. Rubbing the sleep away from my eyes, I sat up and looked around the room. Without warning, I saw a figure stand-ing against the fireplace with a cookie in his hand. Yes, it was one of the cookies from the plate we put out for Santa. Focusing on me was a short man wearing a white shirt and dark pants with black suspenders. He had a white face with a darker beard and matching messy hair.

I stared back at him. And then I started to get excited. "Santa! It's Santa!" I woke my sister and started pointing at the fireplace in the family room excitedly. "Karen, it's Santa!"

Karen sat up and begun to look around the room. "Where, Where!"

Unfortunately, at this point the man had disappeared, but I was still pumped up with excitement. I ran down the hall shrieking at the top of my lungs waking the entire household.

"Santa's here! Santa's here! It's Santa!"

Both my parents and grandparents came into the hall-way to see what all the enthusiasm and eagerness was about. They were annoyed.

"What are you talking about?" my dad said. "Santa isn't here yet. Go back to sleep!"

"No, he was here. I just saw him," I insisted adamantly.

My mom smiled at me, amused by my exuberance.

I started getting frustrated, wondering why none of the adults believed me. "Santa was here," I kept insisting. "He's a short man with suspenders and a black beard!"

At that point, my dad was irritated.

"Santa has a white beard," he said simply. "Go back to sleep."

I replied, "Santa must have been too busy, so he sent his helper."

My mom tucked my sister and me back in bed, but I kept insisting that I had seen Santa or his helper.

Over the next few days, my mom stopped smiling. She knew I hadn't seen Santa. At the same time, she knew I had seen something. At ages where most children started outgrowing Santa, I believed in him because of what I had witnessed that night. It took ten years for my mom to tell me that what I had actually seen was a ghost. When I described him in detail again to her, for the umpteenth time, she brought out a picture that was in storage of her great-uncle from the Civil War era. I was shocked when I saw it! I knew that this was the man I saw on the infamous Christmas Eve so many years ago.

My mom then said, "It is strange how family checks in on us through the years. Family we don't even know or who we are unaware of in the present."

We had a pretty normal childhood with just the two of us, always together, always getting into some mischief. However, my sister would tell me there was something unique about me. It took her a while to figure it out, but she finally said to me "You can see dead people!"

Yes, it really did come down to just that. Can you even begin to imagine the effect that had on two small children? At times, we thought they were monsters coming to get us! When you're waiting for something to come into your house, your senses are heightened. No sound is insignificant. No shadow is friendly. The sound of your own breath terrifies you at any age. In hindsight, I now understand the frustration our parents went through with our stories and always having to check under our beds and inside our closets. It sure made for an interesting childhood, let me tell you!

Pam and Karen in the Summer of 1968

Gradually, I started sharing with my mom more about my past supernatural experiences. In the past, I had wondered if there was something unique in my family line. My grandmother had a gift, my mom had a gift, and now my sister and I had the gift. Who knows how many generations it went back?

To the world, we were just another typical family. My parents were members of the Greatest Generation, with my dad having served in World War II. They met when they were just kids in San Francisco living next door to each other. Our dad had always grown up with his feet planted in reality, which is probably why he found it so difficult to believe the incredible stories of his daughters.

But it wasn't so easy for Dad to dismiss the stories of our mom. Like I said before, our gifts were hereditary. Actually, it even took a long time for our mom to come to terms with her own awareness of her gift. It was one thing for Mom to dismiss our crazy stories, but it was quite another for her to dismiss her own.

When we were young, my mom told us that they went on a Mommy-Daddy weekend to Reno. Mom was spending time in the hotel room while Dad was downstairs at the gambling tables. When my mom sat on the bed, she felt someone sit down right next to her. Looking down, she saw an indentation of buttocks and simultaneously felt the presence of evil. Mom was terrified. She immediately dropped to her knees to pray, asking God to take care of whatever was in the room with her. Slowly, she felt the evil dissipate and eventually joined our Dad.

When my mom used her gift, it could pinpoint negative energy. In the early seventies, as a family we went to check out this huge Victorian home in Petaluma, California. My parents thought this was going to be the home that they had always dreamed of owning. The house was over 150 years old at the time with huge ceilings and gingerbread everywhere. Excitedly, my mom walked into the home, admiring it, but as she walked up to the third floor, she abruptly stopped on the stairs. She felt something was really wrong.

Mom said, "Nope, we have to go," turned and walked back down the stairs and out the front door.

It was a four-hour round-trip drive to Petaluma, and Dad was furious that we had gone all that way, and we never even saw the entire house. Outwardly it was the perfect home for them, what they had been dreaming about for many years. However, Mom would not change her mind. We got in the car and it was dead silent. Finally, Mom said to us that she had felt something scary evil in the house. Dad listened, but being a no-nonsense man of the sixties, he wasn't buying it. Of course, Karen and I did. The moment I walked into the house I absolutely hated it. The feeling of dread was overwhelming. My room would have been on the third floor, where my mom had felt the evil presence. Lucky me!

A year later, my parents tried once again to buy their dream home. At that time, I was thirteen and Karen was eleven years old. It was a beautiful house on Bethel Island located in the California Delta. We were all fishermen, and we loved that the house had a private dock where we could berth our boat. The views of the Delta were outstanding.

Like the first house, the Victorian, this one was huge and picturesque. The house had a substantial wine cellar in the basement where we all headed in that direction to investigate. My dad went down the stairs first, followed by my mom. Suddenly, she felt two strong hands in the middle of her back push her down the stairs. Mom fell three or four steps before she caught herself on the handrail. Immediately we all glanced behind her and saw nothing.

Pam and Karen Fishing During the Summer of 1966

At the end of the home tour, we sat down at the kitchen table with the homeowners and realtor. In advance of negotiations, the homeowners served us refreshments, which consisted of ice-cold glasses of water. At this point, Mom's nerves, were already on edge. Abruptly, the glass of water in front of my mom slid across the table.

No one said a word until Mom said, "What the hell is going on around here?"

The homeowners looked at each other and said, "We have a male Asian ghost who lives here with us, but he's very friendly."

Mom said, "BS, we're leaving now!"

Even though Dad had not seen Mom forcefully pushed down the stairs, he definitely saw the glass of water fly across the kitchen table. We left, ignoring the homeowners' entreaties that the ghost was really, truly friendly, and drove off never to return.

Over the years, our gifts have evolved. My main gift is I see dead people and on occasion feel the energies from the other side. My sister's main gift is feeling the energies from the other side and on occasion seeing the dead people. We laugh because my sister seems to see dead people more often when she is with me. Karen literally sees them hovering around me. Our individual gifts complement each other. Even though there are almost six hundred miles between us, at least once a week, we are able to connect to each other's feelings and thoughts. The gifts act as a bridge between us.

The following stories reflect the hauntings of two sisters tales from adulthood through our early sixties. These are the stories that we have chosen to highlight, our WTH moments; some are funny, some are sad, but they all had a lasting impact on our lives. To this day, we still laugh and cry over them.

Karen and Pam in 1981

*Pam and Karen Celebrating Karen's 60th Birthday
on November 11, 2018*

3

Staircase
from Hell
✝
Karen Pena
1998

W hat do suicidal thoughts over losing a baby, plus a painting of a 17th-century Spanish lady, plus a ghostly apparition of a little girl, plus angels and demons fighting over the soul of a severely depressed woman equal? That's right. You guessed it . . . A staircase from hell!

Finally, it happened. Age thirty-eight and I was pregnant for the first time! Our marriage had never been childless, starting off with two kids (two and four years old) from my husband's previous relationship. However, for nine years we had not used birth control, hoping to have a child together. We were delighted with the results, so much so that I started journaling immediately so our baby would know what a joy she was for us from the moment the very fact of her existence was made known (yes, we were hoping for a little girl).

A few weeks went by and I started to feel some pain in my lower stomach. One day, while I was sitting on the couch, I felt myself being sucked into a vortex of worry and concern about what the pain was about and what it might mean for my condition. And then I heard it, a voice as clear as a bell. Its message consisted of only two clearly spoken words: "Trust me." This was a voice I'd heard before, so I immediately knew who was speaking to me. Even though I knew it was God, however, I figured it wouldn't be a bad idea to have the pain checked out anyway. Finally, I scheduled my first ever visit to a baby doctor. After the examination he told me that my pregnancy was most likely ectopic. In 1998, ultrasound treatments were not all that common like they are today. Rather than ordering one immediately, like he should have done to confirm that my pregnancy was in fact ectopic, he chose to order instead a radioactive shot to kill the fetus in my fallopian tube. Two days later, a nurse, wearing a full body hazmat suit with a long-needled syringe in her hand, entered the small room in which I was waiting, a room that had biohazard warning signs everywhere.

"What the hell?" was all I could think.

The problem was the pregnancy was not in my fallopian tube. It was, on the contrary, exactly where it belonged—in my uterus—a fact that my husband and I were made aware of late that night when he and I went to the Emergency Room after the pain in my stomach had become bad enough to scare us both. The ER doctor performed an ultrasound and assured us that the baby was perfectly okay, but I knew it wasn't because I had already taken the injection.

After being informed of this, she just looked at me and said, "I am so sorry. I don't know how this happened."

I did, though. I had not trusted God. It took three days for my baby to die. I was in Walmart with my sister shopping for cleaning supplies when I felt it start to happen. This is all I want to say about that.

Well, it doesn't take a genius to understand how negative my frame of mind was after going through all this. I was angry and full of pain 24/7, so much so, truth be told, that for the first time in my life I felt suicidal. You see, as a Christian I had failed to trust, and as a result something dark and evil had begun to take advantage of my deep sorrow. Hoping that one day the light of God would return to my so-called life, I felt like a battleground on which God and Satan and their hosts were battling it out.

And this is where this story really begins.

You see, my husband is one of the good ones and he knew that it just wasn't a good idea to wait too long to start coaxing me back into the land of the living. Accordingly, he refused to let up on his attempts to get me back into the hustle and bustle of social life until I finally agreed to spend a whole Saturday out and about on a shopping expedition. We started with an antique shop that had caught my eye before all this started. As soon as we entered the store, I saw it hanging on the back wall: a large oil portrait of a 17th-century Spanish noblewoman. Its appeal was immediate. Maybe it was because of a certain something in her expression, a look of longing, an inconsolable sadness that mirrored what was going on way down in my soul. In other words, she looked like I felt. As it turns out (read on), this artwork may have also been a key to a portal that led to a time warp, a kind of talisman that started a chain reaction that ultimately led to a descent into the netherworld for my whole family. Whatever the reason for its instant appeal, by the end of the day it was hanging in my living room by the staircase, and I got into the habit of stationing myself right in front of it and gazing at it intently. Continuously to mirror her sadness.

One day, when I was making our bed in the master bedroom, I saw a dark shadow out of the corner of my left eye. Assuming it was my husband heading for the hall bathroom, I called out to him. He didn't answer because it wasn't him, which set off a months-long chain of extremely weird incidents.

After my run-in with the shadow, items around the house began to disappear. First it was my daughter´s flip-flops and then her PE clothes, both mysteriously disappearing from where they were sitting on top of the dryer. As if that weren't enough, when I turned on the washing machine it would turn off for no apparent reason. This happened again and again. I brought in a repair person on two different occasions, and both times, after examining it thoroughly, he assured me that there was nothing wrong with it!

At the time, I was taking care of my sick mother. Every night she would take her jewelry off and place it on the night table next to her bed. And then the weirdness decided to approach from another direction; her rings and brooches and everything else she kept in her jewelry box started disappearing, only to be found later in the most unlikely places around the house. (A note of clarification is in order here since some pieces were never found.) After much bewilderment, I finally started to see that whatever was going on was very much out of the ordinary. Ruling out the possibility of burglary—for even though there were some very nice items in Mom´s collection, there was nothing that seemed to be valuable enough to warrant repeated break-ins—I realized that it was time to start thinking outside the box. Now I was on guard, and my attention level was on steroids.

One late night there was a knock on my bedroom door—a very disturbing knock since there was no one in the house except my husband and me, and he was sound asleep right next to me. Before I could begin to process these thoughts and press the proverbial panic button, I heard a little girl outside my door say, "Let me in. Let me in. Why is this door locked?" in a tone of voice that was soft, clear, and precise. Then she knocked again. Then nothing. It had stopped. I thought I was losing my mind. I lay back down, rolled over, and went back to sleep.

But it was not over yet.

The following night, the exact same thing happened. Again, I instinctively turned to my husband, and again, it was obvious—all the more so because of his deafeningly loud snoring—that he was sound asleep and had not heard anything. At this point, it was becoming very obvious to me that these knocks were for my ears alone. It was approximately 2:45 in the middle of the night when I woke up, the darkness in the bedroom relieved by a beam of moonlight streaming in through the window. I knew right away that something was off. I quickly sat up in bed and adjusted my eyes to the dim light. It was then that I looked up and saw her! Right in front of me, at the foot of the bed, was a little girl who looked like she was about six years old. She was dressed in an old-fashioned white nightgown; her hair was streaked with blonde highlights and had a light blue bow in it. My jaw dropped (literally) and I blinked profusely. She was just standing there, staring at me with an innocent look on her face. Although I still don't quite know how to describe what I felt at the time, I've had many years to process my reaction to her appearance, and I am as sure now as I was then that it wasn't fear that I felt. I remembered wondering at the time why this was happening to me and asking myself what in heaven's name she wanted from me. This manifestation occurred night after night, and always her form appeared to me at the same place, right at the foot of my bed. And as always, I was the only one who saw her.

Okay. By now I am an insomniac, lucky to get even three hours sleep a night. I am on high alert, not knowing what's going to happen next. On those long, (almost) sleepless nights, I would typically try to work off the anxiety and the unknown by retreating to our office and paying bills or balancing our checkbook. But I knew I wasn't alone. Sometimes the paper shredder would continuously start, my hand nowhere near the "on" switch, making an industrial grade noise as if it were shredding an entire book. With the house dead silent, I would quietly sit there and just stare at the misbehaving machine, even moving my hand over it like a wand to see if that would make it shut itself off. No luck there. Then I checked the room for some sort of something in the air—a flying bug, maybe?—but no luck in that department, either. The next day I had my husband check it out, and again nothing. Night after night this activity went on with no explanation. Some bat-shit crazy stuff, wouldn't you say?

Soon after this, something else joined the nightly horror show. Any words I could conceivably come up with to describe this new phenomenon seemed hopelessly unreal to me by virtue of its foreignness to my very idea of what is normal. Nonetheless, the show must go on, as they say, so for the sake of this story I will attempt a description (reader patiently waits out long pause while I gather my thoughts).

"She was dressed in an old-fashioned white nightgown; her hair was streaked with blonde highlights and had a light blue bow in it..."

It's 3:00 in the morning, the infamous witching hour when spirits good and bad are closest to us. I am sitting in the office, doing my thing, trying very hard to focus on getting something done (the better to ignore that infernal paper shredder) when all of a sudden the loudest sound advances at a fast clip up the stairs and stops right outside my office door! I still believe that a fair way of describing it would be to compare it to the sound that would be made by a huge parade of elephants, at least a dozen. I started to shake violently from head to toe. What the hell was that? It was certainly nothing that I'd ever experienced—obviously paranormal but way, way beyond any notion of the paranormal I'd had up to that point. This was a WTH moment if there ever was one!

What new supernatural torture was this? Did a band of demons have me in their crosshairs?

The paper shredder and the elephants weren't done with me, subjecting me to a repeat performance of the same old horror show night after night. When I did manage to fall asleep, I would wake up with the little girl standing at the foot of my bed!! What to do now?

I called Mom.

My mother came to stay with us later that week. My husband was unaware of what was going on, and I desperately needed daily emotional support. Although I knew my mom would get it, just how much she would get it was something I would only find out considerably later. I mentioned before that my mom's jewelry had occasionally gone missing, but more than that, she started experiencing the same crazy stuff at night that I was! But Mom being so totally grin-and-bear-it, she kept very quiet about it as it was not something she would choose to burden me with in my stressed out and depressed state.

Sophia, Karen's Blue-fronted Amazon parrot

I had a stunning Blue-fronted Amazon parrot named Sophia. We kept her huge cage downstairs in the corner of the family room. When people were around, Sophia chatted constantly, greeting newcomers with "Hello, Hello." When I approached the cage, she would say "I love you," but what she enjoyed most of all was music and would sing along and dance to the score of *The Phantom of the Opera.* Man, could she dance! At bedtime, I would cover her with a huge yellow blanket. That's how she knew it was quiet time and would refrain from any and all noisemaking afterwards.

Then the angels started showing up.

On one occasion, in the middle of the night, my mom and I met just outside our bedrooms, both of us listening to Sophia saying "Hello" again and again and again. With repetition the volume of her "Hellos" steadily increased, and that's how we both knew that someone (or something) was down there with her next to her cage. We exchanged glances and looked downstairs. All we could see was a supernatural golden glow that expanded outwards from Sophia's cage until it filled the family room. Mom and I both knew this was indeed something very special, an angelic encounter, and could see that Sophia was delighted to be in the center of this great big cloud of spiritual happiness. As for myself, all I could feel was the joy that comes with once again wearing a (badly needed) smile on my heart.

During this emotion-packed period, my sister would sometimes come and keep me company. She would sleep downstairs on the couch, right next to Sophia. Often, in the morning, she would inform me that she was awakened by an unnerving feeling, a feeling so strong that at times she was afraid even to open her eyes. For the sake of my sister's peace of mind, Mom and I decided to keep her out of the loop regarding the goings-on in the house until much, much later.

Soon after, at around 2:00 one afternoon, my daughter Tianna came out of her bedroom and stood at the top of the stairs. I happened to be standing in the office doorway, waiting to see if she needed something. She started to say something to me, and then it happened. She tumbled down the stairs, landing on her stomach in the landing area with her head crashing into the front wall so hard that the top half of it ended up inside the hole it had just made! I stood there in the office door, so badly shocked that I couldn't move at first. Then I just ran, almost knocking over my husband who had raced to the landing at the same time. Badly shaken and upset, my daughter was all right—thank God.

She looked at us and said, "Who pushed me?"

Although I could hardly identify the culprit by name, I knew, nonetheless, that she had been pushed by some evil unseen force—the same evil force that had been haunting me for months. And this brings me to the next portion of my story.

So now my kids were being affected by the evil I had brought into the house. Was it my suicidal thoughts? The painting? Both? What I haven't told you yet is that the little girl I mentioned earlier wasn't alone anymore. Although I had known for a while that there was a strange man in her vicinity, I wasn't aware of him at first. Months went by before he actually registered in my field of vision. The first look I got of him was of his reflection in the bathroom mirror while doing my morning beauty routine, getting ready for the day. He looked like the counterpart to the woman in the oil painting, belonging to the same historical time frame as she. He had very white skin and long, wavy black hair stopping just below his shoulders. His eyebrows were dark and dramatic, and his eyes were even darker, matching in color the thin black mustache that curled up at the ends. He was wearing a red velvet jacket with a white shirt with ruffles around the neck and wrists. He wore a wide black belt with an oversized silver buckle holding up a pair of loose-fitting black pants that were tucked into knee-high black leather boots. As crazy as it sounds, he looked very much like—or at least like the picture I had in mind that came from watching tv reruns of 1930s-1940s Hollywood blockbusters—a Spanish nobleman.

"He had very white skin and long, wavy black hair stopping just below his shoulders…"

WTH was going on!

One thing I knew for sure is that I did not understand the connection between the Nobleman and the little girl who was coming into my room at night. As this uncertainty grew, my numbness increased. I figured I just had to accept the fact that as crazy and grotesque as the situation had become, this is my life now and what can I do about it? I felt like a complete idiot because of my powerlessness-fueled complacency.

One evening at around midnight, I had a horrible nightmare. My uninvited guest had his white sweaty palms around my neck and was trying to choke the life out of me. He was standing over me with an expression on his face that was so evil that I screamed at the top of my lungs. In the nightmare, I was struggling and pulling as hard as I could at his hands to break their death grip on my throat. At the same time, I felt excruciating pressure on my chest, so excruciating that my lungs were burning! I let go of his hands, and as I frantically flailed my arms everywhere, I knocked everything off of my nightstand. As I heard the items falling to the floor, I could feel the life force slowly draining from my exhausted body. Despite what people have told me about the impossibility of dying in a nightmare, I realized then and there that they could quite possibly be wrong.

I was in the fight of my life, but then as abruptly as this nightmare began, it ended with my assailant quickly releasing his hands from my neck and disappearing. I gasped and treated myself to a much needed long deep breath! My heart, which seemed to be hell-bent on pounding itself right out of my chest, slowly calmed down after a considerable amount of time had gone by and I was eventually able to go back to (a very unrestful) sleep. Before that, I looked to my right to see if my husband had been disturbed at all: again, sound asleep.

When I awoke that morning, I quietly lay there thinking long and hard about the hideous nightmare I just had, a nightmare so frightful that just thinking about it caused my heart to beat faster. The horror increased when I glanced over at the floor and saw everything that I'd knocked off my nightstand. And that's when I knew, at that precise moment, that it was anything but a nightmare. No, this wasn't a dream. It had really happened. Strangely enough, though, this very dark cloud turned out to have just the silver lining that I needed.

Finally, the time had come to confide in my sister Pam. When I told her what was going on, she was a little skeptical at first. She believed that something out of the ordinary was happening, but really, a "parade of elephants" thundering up the stairs? Really now?! She insisted that there had to be a logical explanation! After talking for weeks about it, she finally decided to come down and spend the night, and in this way, she could see for herself what was going on. I arranged for my two kids to spend the night with their friends so that my sister and her husband could occupy one of the kids' bedrooms while our mom occupied the other.

Pam's Old English Sheepdog, Watson

My sister brought her Old English Sheepdog Watson with her and made a cozy little nest for him in my downstairs laundry room. My sister's and mom's rooms were right at the top of the stairs. After having a nice dinner and evening together we got ready for bed. My sister Pam, ever the daredevil, told me that she was not going to take it if the ghost started anything. Instead, after some deliberation and heartfelt prayer, she decided that she was ready to read the proverbial riot act to these ghouls. Although my husband and I had our bedroom door closed and locked, my sister and mom decided to leave their doors open. After all, they wanted to be sure they could hear everything. By 11:00 p.m., we were all fast asleep. At about 2:00 a.m., my sister was awakened by the sound of her dog shaking his head down in the laundry room, which caused his collar to make an extremely disturbing rattling sound. This was followed by the sound of Sophia saying, "Hello, Hello, Hello."

Suddenly, the dreadful noise of the parade of elephants thundering up the stairs and into my sister's bedroom began. All she could think to do was to bury her head in the pillow, hoping that by doing so she could erase the very reality of whatever it was that was standing right next to her by that time. Realizing that her head was so deep in the pillow that she couldn't breathe, she managed to put enough distance between her face and the pillow to take in some badly needed oxygen. After shaking her husband awake, she broke out in hysterical sobbing. A river of tears flowed from her cheeks, as the situation overwhelmed her with its sheer and unmitigated randomness. She then yelled out to Mom in the next room and asked her if she'd heard what just happened.

Mom replied in the affirmative.

With Mom as her witness, my sister told her husband, who had somehow managed to sleep through the entire incident, what had just happened. Both ladies then retreated to the bathroom, where my sister continued to sob over what had just happened. Suddenly, there was the sound of a man screaming outside the bathroom door.

Pam said, "Shhh, shhh, do you hear that?" and opened the bathroom door to see what was going on. There at the top of the staircase was my sister's husband telling whatever it was to back off and get its ugly behind back home to hell! By now the whole house was awake and my sister was too immobilized by what she'd just been through to assist her husband in his valiant efforts!

This was all too much for my sister, and first thing in the morning she started flipping through the Yellow Pages looking for some kind of help. After a bit of research and much discussion, she called a paranormal investigation team that came to one's house and spent the night with cameras and tape recorders activated. They seemed thankful for the opportunity and agreed to pencil us in for their first available time slot. By the way, back then, unlike today, very few people were doing this.

Finally, the big night arrived. As much as we dreaded what we might find out, we were, at the same time, actually excited by the prospect of someone capturing and recording events. Again, we bundled up the kids and sent them over to their friend's house for the night. The crew arrived at around 10:00 p.m., gear in hand. After they'd spent an hour or so setting up everything, we gathered in a completely darkened living room and waited for something to happen. After an entire evening spent waiting patiently, the camera crew was able to capture some very strange noises on the stairwell which focused on the side by the large antique oil portrait of a 17th-century Spanish noblewoman. It also managed to capture something extremely creepy and thoroughly freaky—a staircase temperature reading of 66.6 degrees Fahrenheit! The rest of the house was at 78 degrees Fahrenheit.

The next morning, I brought up to my sister that she should take the painting and try hanging it up in her staircase at home to see what happens. Her immediate response, let's just say, cannot be printed in this book. So, I took the painting outside and took a knife to it, cutting it into many pieces followed by setting it on fire and watching it burn to ashes.

So, there you have it: the indescribable sadness that comes from losing a baby, the suicidal depression that lasted months, demons and angels fighting over my tortured soul while I fought my hardest to keep mind intact. The numerous supernatural horrors that had turned our house into a freak show from hell and a painting of a woman that could have been me and whose fallen state so clearly resembled mine that I just had to have it—until I destroyed it utterly in an attempt to exorcise whatever bad energy it had projected back onto me.

Our cozy domicile had turned into a paranormal crime scene.

A little while later, we sold the house.

Be it ever forgotten, there's no place like home.

I was awakened abruptly by a sound from somewhere in the house. It was one of those sounds you could not put your finger on, but it was enough to wake me up out of a sound sleep. I glanced at the clock on my nightstand, which said 3:05 a.m. For a brief moment, I just lay there quietly in the dark. I might have even held my breath. As still as a mummy, I listened intently for that noise that had given me such a strangely odd feeling. My first thought was someone was trying to break in the house downstairs, but our dogs did not make a sound or react in any way. I looked up into the dark in front of me. We kept our bedroom pitch black, without so much as a night light to offset the darkness.

Again, I knew something wasn't right, and the negative knot in my stomach was increasing.

I sat up ramrod straight on the edge of our bed and placed my feet solidly on the floor. Suddenly, there was a flash of movement of something darker than dark taking two steps back. It was at that point I realized it had been only fifteen inches or so from my face. As it stood there looking down on me, I had the opportunity to get a good look at it. There stood this over six-foot-tall, solid, slender Spiderman figure with the longest arms and fingers I had ever seen, and to make this stranger-than-strange creature look even worse, it was holding his arms straight down, directly by its side flexing his long, creepy fingers.

"…it was holding his arms straight down, directly by its side flexing his long, creepy fingers…"

I was horror-struck! The panic that overcame me literally took my breath away and paralyzed my entire body. It took a few moments for me to gain my composure. I immediately took a deep breath so I would not black out with this creature standing directly in front of me. It just stood there, looking straight at me. I then let out a scream that was sufficiently horrifying to jolt my soundly sleeping husband into a sitting position with a look of astonishment on his face that I will never, ever forget.

The Spiderman immediately vanished, disappearing in a flash. I could barely get the words out of my mouth to describe to my husband what had just occurred. WTH was that? I had never seen anything like that before! I believed I had just seen my first demon. To make matters worse, I had an overwhelming urge to pee right then and there. There was no way I was going by myself; my husband had to escort me.

Let's click the reset button and start from the beginning with the—let's just say—weird, spooky, and inexplicable events that led up to this terrifying night.

Nine months earlier is when we started to notice things. At first, these incidents weren't alarming and were few and far between. With our busy lifestyle, we didn't give these occurrences much thought, chalking them up instead to the wind, the dogs, the house settling on its foundation. We'd considered all these things, but the one thing we never, ever considered was that there was anything supernatural about them.

My husband and I both worked outside the home, and I was always the first to return home from work.

And then it began.

I started to feel a strange and uneasy feeling as soon as I opened the front door and turned the lights on. At first it didn´t happen every day, just occasionally. But then it started to escalate. I began to pay more attention, and I mean a lot more attention, to this feeling. Chalking it up to the wind, dogs, or just the house settling no longer made sense. I just knew beyond a doubt that there was an energy in the house, hiding somewhere. The first time I felt it, I let our dogs in and watched them very carefully to see if they were guided by that celebrated doggie ESP to a particular place in the house. It was business as usual for them, however. The only object of their attention, as always, was Mommy, who was greeted with the usual burst of excitement reserved for parental homecomings. At that point I decided to roll up my sleeves and get to work on cracking this case, initiating a daily routine of inspecting every room and closet (and even the showers) to check for the intruder that I just knew was there. The results of that surveillance were always negative, and I just chalked it all up to my imagination. My husband, knowing what an Investigation Discovery (ID) Channel junkie I was—guilty as charged, your honor—suggested that I just might be watching that channel just a wee bit too much!

A few months later, we went to Hawaii on a planned vacation and left our friend's son in charge of watching our home for us. On the second night away, we received a frantic call from him telling us that he felt someone's presence in the house. We told him to do an inspection tour while we stayed on the phone with him. Searching every nook and cranny, he found nothing or no one. That still did not satisfy him, and his fear continued to grow, along with his conviction that someone or something was keeping him company! Concerned about his emotional state, we called a friend and asked him to go over to check things out and spend some time with him until he felt comfortable again. It apparently worked, and there were no further distress calls from him while we were away on vacation.

It was, however, by no means over. When we returned back from our vacation, this feeling of someone being in the house began to happen on a daily basis. There were times I would call a family friend who only lived about a mile away. He was always happy to come over and check the house out for me on those days when this feeling got the best of me. Sometimes when I got home, I would sit in my car in the driveway for a while, afraid to go inside because I just knew that that bad feeling was going to be there. That bad feeling was so strong, it was unbelievable! I would look around the neighborhood and wonder if anyone else had ever experienced this, and if not, why was it happening to us? Why couldn't I just be normal and just get out of my car and walk in the house without feeling or sensing evil? I thought this bad feeling had to be something evil because it was not at all a good feeling. After requesting his help several times, I began to suspect that my friend might think that I needed either to be on meds or see a therapist, or (better yet) both! Perhaps because he could so easily see the look of terror on my face, however, he was always very kind about it, and if he had any reservations about my mental state, chose to keep them to himself.

And then things really started to escalate, with shadows in our peripheral vision, figures in the dark, footsteps, noises, knocking sounds, doors slamming, and that constant feeling that someone was watching us!

My husband would tell me he saw a tall shadow out of the corner of his eye. A few days later, I started to see this shadow. I saw it mostly coming down the staircase. It was always out of the corner of our eye, and that led us to question ourselves. Did we really see it or was it just the lighting playing tricks on our vision? Maybe, in fact, it was just my imagination succumbing to fear and fatigue. One thing that was beyond a reasonable doubt, in any case, was that this whole thing was getting weirder and creepier by the minute! I hated being home. The home we spent so much time remodeling and making just the way we wanted terrified me! Several times the feeling was so strong that I asked my husband to call in sick and stay home with me.

One night my husband was upstairs and I was downstairs when, at the exact same moment, we heard each other's name called. He came downstairs as I headed up, both of us asking the other what they wanted. Incidents like this, things that just could not be rationally explained, were happening more frequently. All I could think about was what was going to happen next? My husband, on the other hand, was making a lot of excuses and didn't seem at all to be taking it as seriously as I was. At least that is what I thought, until one night, when we went to bed, I noticed my husband's rosary beads hanging on the bedpost on his side, and I knew right then and there that he believed more than he was admitting to.

Then one morning, our overnight guest came down for breakfast and told me about the unbelievably creepy thing that had happened to him during the night. While lying in bed, he was treated to a rear view of a big black dog walking around his bed. At first, he thought it was our dog, our beloved dark gray Old English Sheepdog. The thing of it was, though, how had he gotten through that closed door? The next thing he knew was that this thing, this almost-dog thing, was on his bed and paw imprints started making their way up the blanket towards his head. Paralyzed by fear, he just lay there, waiting to see what was going to happen next. Once it reached him, however, it disappeared into thin air. After hearing about this, I was now sure—as sure as I needed to be—that we had something in our home, something that was obviously not a good thing. I believe in my heart our guest just might have seen a hellhound, like the kind you hear about, the kind you might read about in books or see in movies. But to think they could be real! OMG.

"...this thing, this almost-dog thing, was on his bed and paw imprints started making their way up the blanket.."

The mood in our home began to change, as did the nitty-gritty of daily life. It seemed that there were more and more arguments, and simple disagreements often intensified into dramatic fights. There was a depressed feeling throughout our home. Emotions were on high alert, and in the meantime, something had—at least temporarily—cancelled the love, laughter, and happiness that had been in our lives.

During the next several months I would see huge insects, black in color, half a dozen at a time, resembling grasshoppers with four legs and ranging from around one to two feet long, walking up the walls and across the ceiling of our bedroom. I tended to believe it was my imagination, a reflection, or my eyes playing tricks on me. The one thing I *never* thought—or at least never dared to think—was that I was actually, really seeing them. This was just as terrifying, if not more than Spiderman because I hate bugs! One night I actually felt the sensation of being held down in my bed and choked so hard that I couldn't breathe! Terrified by the feeling of not being able to get loose, I went into a full-size panic!

Was someone trying to kill me?

What on earth was going on?

We started hearing knocks on our bedroom doors and even on our bedposts. Heading to a room and having the door slam right in our face just before we entered fast became a familiar experience. This was so bad that our housekeeper, who had been with us for over three years, suddenly quit. In her phone message, she said that we needed our home blessed because there is something really bad in it! Finally, after all the shock and horror, the climax came in the form of the shadow man standing right over me one night until my bolting upright from a prone position caused him to take two steps back and vanish. That is when we decided to have our home blessed by a clergyman, firmly convinced that a truckload of good prayers and an ocean of holy water were just what we needed at that point.

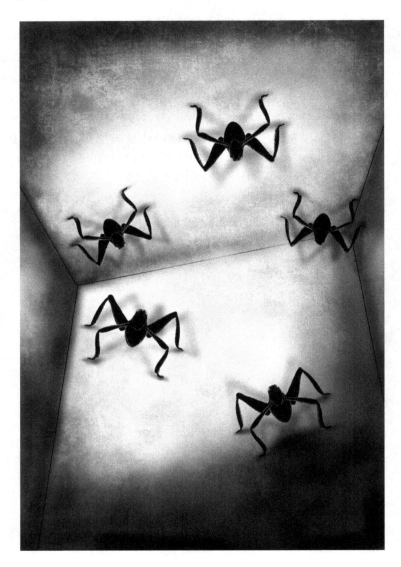

"...huge insects, black in color, half a dozen at a time, resembling grass-hoppers with four legs and ranging from around one to two feet long..."

Things finally did calm down a little after we'd had our home blessed. Eventually, these incidents were actually few and far between. Considering what we'd gone through, it would be understandable if you thought that this might have been a good time to break out the champagne and do a few victory laps, but that was hardly the case. Sadly enough, I never felt quite the same about our home, and continued to harbor a bad taste in my mouth that just would not go away. The fact of the matter is that I never again felt safe there, and never again wanted to be alone in that house. To make it worse, whatever it was that had shaken up our lives so thoroughly hadn't quite said "Aloha" yet, never abandoning us, unfortunately, for long periods of time and checking in with us every so often. We had gone years and years with not one unpleasant surprise in that house, and all of a sudden something so creepy and unbelievable starts out of nowhere!

I could never get over what had happened. I could never feel safe there again. I could never be alone in the house. And the biggest thing, I could NEVER sleep in the dark again, always having to have a nightlight right by my bedside. Eventually we sold our home and moved far away, never to return.

What caused the energy in the house to change suddenly after three years of peace and normalcy? It wasn't until sixteen years later when déjà vu occurred that we made the connection. A friend's friend who had stayed with us during that time, unbeknownst to us, had a dark side dabbling into witchcraft. There is no doubt in my mind that the two occurrences were connected.

5

A Graveyard
too Close for
Comfort

✝

Pam Mandel

2008

Have you ever thought of what it would be like to
live next door to a graveyard? Truth be told, I can't
even remember the moment at which my brain
threatened to shut down after hearing a friend ask for the
umpteenth time if we'd ever seen or heard a ghost. The
other comment on the chart was, "Doesn't living near a

THE HAUNTINGS OF TWO SISTERS

graveyard creep you out?" And then (drum roll please), just to lighten the mood a bit, the wittiest of them would chime in with something like, "At least your neighbors are quiet, with the exception of an occasional gravedigger!"

My husband and I had moved from the Bay Area to Las Vegas to help care for my elderly parents after my father was given only a short time to live. That way, we would have more time to spend with him while also being closer to our family. After a few years, Dad passed, and we decided to move back to where I have lived my entire life—the San Francisco Bay Area. Since we wanted to take our time finding a home to purchase, we decided to rent a place for a year or two until we found something that met our requirements. What we did need was a landlord or landlady who loved animals and would accept our furry menagerie—not an easy task when you have three dogs!

The Spooky Graveyard Across the Street

Finally, after hours spent searching online, eureka! There it was, the perfect two-story, 3,000-square-foot home with four bedrooms, three baths, and a backyard for the dogs to run and play in. The clincher for us consisted of just two words that were included in the ad: "pet friendly." We immediately wondered, however, if that meant only one dog. Would they consider more? Not wanting to miss out on what might be a really good opportunity, I emailed the contact person. A very nice young woman immediately responded to my email with a phone call. She assured us that she had no problem with our having three dogs, even going so far as to say that they, too, loved animals and agreed that this would be the perfect home for us.

Then she added, "We live right across the street from a cemetery, is that okay with you?"

My reply (yes, I do sarcasm): "As long as they are all dead, we are good with it."

We then signed the lease, sight unseen, and got ready for our move back to the area where I was born and raised.

From our new home, you could see the cemetery from just about every window. The house was situated, in fact, just across the street from the entrance. One day I was sitting on the porch looking at it when I realized that my ex-husband's families were all buried there. A creepy thought, you may well say, but for some strange reason I actually felt somewhat comforted by it.

This graveyard was definitely not a small churchyard with only a few headstones. On the contrary, it was massive, and this fact proved to be a bit annoying because of the many funerals that took place there. Funeral = lots of cars = lots of mourners lining the streets blocking traffic several times a week. Granted, otherwise—at least most of the time—the cemetery was very quiet, offering up just an occasional sound or two unless you were actually traipsing through it after dark.

You would think that people buried in the cemetery would not care if you have a party or leave your garbage cans out a day extra after garbage pickup. Really, though, why would they? But let me tell you—there is a big difference between visiting a cemetery and living right next door to one!

Sure, they are all dead. That's why they're there, right?

That's what we thought, too, at first.

Soon after we got settled in, I started to hear footsteps during the night, accompanied by the sound of someone whispering. This was soon followed by the sight of a hat-wearing shadow man peeking around corners and occasionally passing right by me. By the way, all this happened right after my dad passed and my mom would come and stay with us for weeks at a time. Several times I would hear her say out loud, "Pam is that you?" It was not, and no one else was in the house but the two of us. On another occasion I was sitting on the couch reading a book, television off, and I could see the reflection in the TV screen of someone walking behind me. I quickly turned to see who was there and there was no one.

I began to share these experiences with my husband, but he just blew me off.

That is, until now.

Nighttime.

The front door opened so hard that it slammed into the wall. My husband screamed, "Something is chasing us."

Let me start from the beginning, about thirty minutes earlier . . .

When walking our Old English Sheepdog, my husband was in the habit of taking a shortcut through the cemetery in order to get to the field on the other side. Although most nights he set out just before dusk, on this particular one he'd gotten a late start. Not realizing that it would be dark before he got back, he'd forgotten to bring his flashlight with him. As he and doggie were strolling through the dark graveyard on their way back home, they heard a scraping sound pierce the air fewer than twenty feet away. Upon hearing it, his immediate (and exclusive) thought, as he later confided to me, was "What the hell was that?" He listened intently, hearing footsteps and other noises getting closer and closer. Quickly deciding that this was no time to play Sherlock Holmes and locate the sound's source, he started to walk faster and faster.

Unfortunately, so did whoever/whatever was following them.

Both parties picked up the pace, shifting to high gear until they were running so fast that it was a race to see who could get out the gate of the graveyard first! My husband made it in record time, not stopping until he—fur-friend in tow—ran through the front doorway yelling, "Something is chasing us!" The next words out of his mouth, spoken with the utmost conviction, were "NO MORE NIGHT STROLLS THROUGH THE CEMETERY!"

He kept his promise.

Our list of must-haves for a new home suddenly a lot

shorter, we moved out right after our one-year lease was up. Graveyards can be haunted to the point where they are too, too spooky for words, and we vowed that we would never live next to one again—a vow that we have never broken.

KAREN'S EXPERIENCE OF THE GRAVEYARD

When I heard that my sister had moved next to a graveyard, I just couldn't believe it, yet here we are, my mom and I, spending the week here visiting.

I am seated at the kitchen counter, with a full view of the family room. I am just hanging out there, having a soda and a warm family-style chat.

And then I see it . . . my first demon that actually looks like a demon!

It enters the kitchen through the sliding glass door, from the direction of the graveyard, walking across the room and disappearing—but not before stopping right in front of me and staring at me long and hard, like it knew I was watching it.

This particular demon was black, blacker than black, blacker than the darkest night. With a body that was thin and extremely bony and eyes a whitish-gray, it was walking briskly but erratically, as if it had bad knees or something. The minute I saw it, a feeling of dread came over me, a feeling that ran so deep that it spared neither body nor soul. Shocking as it was, the biggest surprise of all, perhaps, was that no one else saw it! I'm looking at the faces of my family members, and no one is reacting to this but me! I guess it was for my eyes only. Typical demon experience because now I'm the crazy one, right?

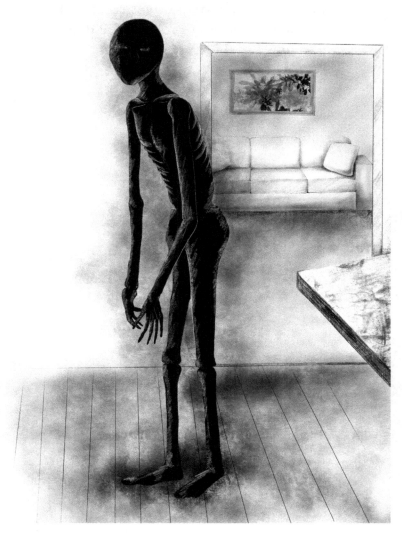

"With a body that was thin and extremely bony and eyes a whitish-gray, it was walking briskly but erratically…"

Howard,
I'm Home!
✝
Pam Mandel
2013 - 2018

When my husband and I decided to purchase a vacation house for short getaways, our one non-negotiable requirement was that we all, including our three dogs, would feel right at home. We finally found a nice little northern California lakeside cottage, which, after being treated to a generous helping of TLC, promised to be a cozy little nest for all species involved!

This cottage sat right on the water with its own dock and a huge deck that included a retractable awning. The yard was so private, surrounded by mature trees and hundreds of flowering bulbs. The previous owner had a real green thumb! With its panoramic view, we could just see ourselves sitting on the dock with our dogs and fishing poles.

One of the main focal points of the yard were the numerous birdhouses throughout the property. Every birdhouse was occupied by a family of at least five birds. The harmony of birds singing as they did their daily chores infiltrated every part of the yard. This turned your morning coffee by the firepit into a gorgeous symphony.

We quickly settled into a happy routine, going up there for long weekends twice a month. Our little hideaway just as quickly turned out to be doggie heaven, and my husband and I loved to treat ourselves to the sight of our dogs jumping off the dock, swimming after the ducks, and chasing after the flying toys that we threw in the water for them. All in all, it was our happy place, a place of ample rest and reprieve where we created priceless memories for ourselves.

A high point of the summer season was a week-long visit from my sister and her grandkids. For them it seemed like a veritable Disney World of warm weather fun, with a daily diet of fishing, knee-boarding, and swimming—all of it washed down with a barrelful of laughter. Not having grandchildren of our own, spending that week with them was something we looked forward to all year long.

About two years after we purchased the place, my mom and I went there to ring in the new year with the expectation that my husband would join us in a few days. And then the new year decided to come in with a bang—a great, big, horrific, supernatural bang that I couldn't have, for the life of me, even begun to anticipate. And it didn't even wait for New Year's Eve! In fact, it all started on December 29 at 10:05 p.m., a date and time that will forever be tattooed on my mind. I was sitting alone in the living room on our couch, just hanging out and watching TV. My mom had retired early for the evening, so the house was very quiet. Suddenly, out of the right corner of my eye, about ten feet away, I saw a light-bathed foggy white mist begin to form. It quickly grew denser and darker. While the question replayed itself in my mind—what the hell is this?—it was quickly answered in the form of a man just standing there and looking at me so intensely that I was completely taken aback.

Who or what on earth was this? He was an older man in his early eighties. His clothes consisted of a red and black long-sleeved plaid flannel shirt and beige khaki pants, capped off with a black belt and shoes of a dark hue. He stood perfectly still with both arms held straight down at his side, all the while staring directly at me with an expression that can be fairly described as dark and menacing.

*"He stood perfectly still with both arms held straight down at his side,
all the while staring directly at me.."*

And then I did something that I thought was very brave. I turned my head slightly, just enough so that I looked directly at him. Imagine my surprise when at that moment—just when our eyes locked—he immediately vanished! I attempted to stay calm. I reminded myself that I'd just had eye surgery and maybe I was prone to find myself in a predicament in which what I actually saw was something completely different. I assured myself (or tried to) that it was probably nothing at all, certainly not something that warranted further thought.

Unfortunately, I just couldn't manage to get this out of my mind. How could my eyes, in their weakened post-op state, treat me to a spectacle that was as clear and as vivid as what I'd just seen? I was completely shaken and couldn't seem to help myself. I thought it best to keep this to myself rather than sharing it with my mom. After all, there was no need to scare her and make her feel uncomfortable.

Early the next morning, my sister called for our daily morning chat to see how our mom was doing. I was in the middle of giving her an update on Mom's health when I decided to change the subject. Instead, I started to give her a blow-by-blow description, almost laughingly, about the experience I had had the previous night with the Old Man. I told her the entire story, leaving out nothing except a description of his wardrobe. I ended the conversation by concluding that I was either crazy or my eyesight was worsening to the point where another operation was forthcoming.

My sister asked, in a very calm voice, if he'd been wearing a red and black long-sleeved plaid flannel shirt with beige khaki pants?

I replied, "Yes."

She then said, "You are not crazy."

What I couldn't grasp was this: how in the world could she have possibly known what this man was wearing while I was having doubts as to whether or not I had even really seen him? I finally managed to ask her how she could have possibly known what he was wearing.

"Because, Pam," she replied, "I have seen him twice now while visiting with you."

Okay, now things were getting seriously creepier by the minute. I asked her why she hadn't shared this with me before.

She replied with, "It's really simple—you love it up there so much I didn't want to ruin your time at the lake house."

After a long, stunned silence on the phone, I finally got up the nerve to ask her where she had seen this man. She said that the first time had been on Easter Sunday when her grandchildren were visiting. We were having an Easter egg hunt in the yard, and our Man was down by the front gate, bent over one of the flower beds in which he was hard at work with his gardening. The second time she saw him was at about 2:00 in the morning. She'd been in bed, looking out the bedroom door, when she spied him walking down the hall towards the master bedroom carrying something. Upon hearing his destination, I thought "OMG, that is where *we* were sleeping!" Although she couldn't exactly see for sure what it was, she was able to make out that whatever he was carrying was something heavy and box-like. She also informed me that the first time she had visited the lake house, his energy was standing right outside the guest room door. She immediately felt a strong surge of spiritual energy coming from him while having the sensation of walking right through him.

I was overwhelmed by her story, trying like mad to wrap my mind around all that she had just told me. A pause followed another pause that followed an even longer pause. And then it screamed itself out of my mouth:

"OMG, I have a GHOST here, too?"

My sister just laughed and said, "Duh, Pam."

After getting off the phone with her, I began thinking back on the two and a half years since we had purchased the home. What both my sister and I had experienced explained so, so much—especially the many occasions after dark when I was working at my computer, feeling so strongly that I was being watched that I ended up with goosebumps up and down my arms. Every time that happened, I would check all of the outside security cameras to see if anyone had been spying on me. Truth be told, some nights I would become so upset and frightened that I would hurry to our bed and cuddle with my husband. My instincts were letting me know that something strange was going on in this cottage.

Often, the sound of dishes being washed in the kitchen at all hours of the night accompanied the sound of soft slippers sliding *shish shish* across the kitchen and bathroom floors. Occasionally we heard late-night knocks at the front door with no one standing there. Kayaking by our dock, our neighbors from down the road saw an older man wave to them from our deck. They turned around to wave back at him, and he was gone. It was all beginning to make sense now. So many situations that I had not understood, so many situations that conjured up a definite WTH moment.

Once more, OMG, I now had a ghost at our vacation home!

Now I was on a mission to find out who this ghost was, why he was here, and what he wanted. I started thinking about the actual identity of this ghost. Who could he be? Was he attached to the land, or to the house, or to both? If I spoke to him, would he hear me? Even though the thought of it terrified me, would I see him again? I was desperate to find out who this ghost was.

Wouldn't you be at this point?

Then I remembered my sister saying to me she felt that the energy she was feeling in the house was the previous owner of the property.

I then recalled the fact that we had purchased the house from an elderly widow whose husband had recently passed, I couldn't help but think, "Oh, Lord, could my sister be right? Had her husband gone to his eternal reward in the beautiful lake house that I so loved? Was this him?" I searched our makeshift home office frantically to find our closing papers. After what seemed like an eternity had passed, I found them.

Her husband's name was Howard. He had passed in his eighties, a fact that fit perfectly with the age of the ghost. "Close, but no cigar," I thought. I needed more— preferably a picture. Nothing less would make this case airtight! I spent hours online, Googling here, there, and everywhere for a picture of this guy. Alas, nothing came up, not even an obituary with a picture. At that crucial moment, it looked like I had hit a dead end.

Yes, I felt discouraged, but not to the point where I wanted to throw in the towel. My husband and I were headed up to the lake house that weekend, and I was determined to take the investigation up a notch by quizzing a neighbor who had lived next door for years. Certainly, he had to have known Howard and what he had looked like. We invited him over for coffee and every so often threw in a few questions about Howard. What did he look like? Was he a nice guy? What did he like to wear? Our neighbor looked a little confused but ultimately was able to answer all of our questions about Howard's appearance. He admitted that I'd described Howard's looks pretty darn accurately.

Like all reasonable people, my husband and I decided to extend the utmost congeniality to our new housemate. I would be doubly sure to kick off long weekends at the house with a warm and effusive "Howard, I'm home!" which I thought would help work off some stress. What I soon discovered was that Howard was not amused. Calling him out only made him pay more attention to me, and not in a good way. It was the kind of attention one might receive from a stalker.

Soon after, my sister saw him working in the garden again. This kind of made sense, horticulture obviously being Mr. Howard's favorite hobby. Looking into Howard's life kicked off a whole new round of activity. At that point I had ample reason to believe that he was anything but a happy camper—so unhappy, in fact, that on one occasion an attempt to engage Howard in friendly fashion ended with a can of tuna fish flying across a crowded room.

Once we took my sister's grandkids, Carl and Amy, out on the boat knee-boarding that afternoon, leaving our mom at home to watch the doggies. After we returned and came in the house to check on our mom, she asked my sister why we didn't take Amy with us.

Karen said, "We did, Mom."

Mom said, "No, you didn't. She was sitting in that chair."

Karen started to ask her questions. Bottom line, Mom asked the little girl questions, but she never replied. Mom thought at the time that it was very strange but never dreamed it was a ghost.

When I heard the story, I thought, "OMG, another one resides here!"

One morning at around 6:00, I woke up and went to get coffee. I saw my sister through the patio window. She was having her morning cigarette. I went to stick my head out the patio door to say hi, but when I tried to open it, it was locked. After opening it, I asked Karen why she had used the front door. She said she didn't.

I said, "How did you get outside?"

She said, "I came out the patio door, but then someone had locked me out."

Not believing her, I thought she might have gone out the front door, so I took a look myself and saw that it, too, was locked. I was amazed to say the least. I didn't know who just yet, but someone was playing a game with this patio door.

The next morning, I got up before anyone and went to let the dogs out. I noticed that the patio door was open about two inches and immediately asked my husband and sister why they left the door unlocked and open. They said they didn't, that they hadn't even been out there yet. Being skeptical, I did not believe them. So that night I did the final round to make sure the patio door was locked before going to bed. Guess what? The next morning the patio door was again opened and unlocked the same way. Being the ID Channel junkie I am, I was horrified! How could I sleep knowing that this door might not be locked? A simple solution came to mind immediately. I had our handyman come out to the house that day and install another lock at the bottom of the patio door. It was up in the air whether the ghost would just unlock both, but it never did.

One night, Carl and Amy decided, flashlight in hand, to start asking Howard questions. Our invisible friend was asked to respond by switching the flashlight on for "yes" and switching it off for "no."

No dice.

What we did get, however, was the flashlight flying across the room, hitting me right in the hip. Bad quickly went to worse as Amy ran out of the house, bawling her precious head off hysterically! Howard had plainly demonstrated by now that he was less than thrilled with us.

My husband's brother and his wife decided to come for a visit, and we all decided to meet at our lake house. During their first night, Michael's sister-in-law could not sleep, so she decided to go out to the living room on the couch. After falling asleep, she was awakened by the feeling of someone standing directly over her. Too afraid to open her eyes, she turned over and faced the wall. A few minutes later, that feeling of being watched disappeared. The next morning, she shared her feelings of what had happened, and I then told her of some of my experiences, the same ones I am sharing with you.

I got the bright idea to rearrange our bedroom furniture so that the bed was closer to the TV. At the time, I did not realize that I would have a full view of the hallway from my bed when the bedroom door was open. This was a situation I would soon regret. One night, while glancing down the hall, I saw the top of a body moving four feet in front of the bottom half, as if it were stretched out like a rubber band. Eventually the bottom reconnected with the top. I was so shocked, then I realized it was Howard going from the front door to the kitchen.

Now this is going to sound really crazy. One day, I was at our main home and wanted to check on our vacation house. I occasionally checked the security cameras since we're not always there. When I reached the camera that showed the dock, I saw Howard standing at the end of the dock looking out at the water. Suddenly he put his arms straight up in the air and simultaneously his entire body was sucked up into a ball of light! His apparition turned into an orb in front of the camera and flew off across the water. Crazy, I know, but I couldn't believe my eyes! This was a WTH moment!

Now things were about to get even nuttier.

On hot nights at the lake house, our eighty-pound goldendoodle Dexter loved to sleep right by the front door on the cool tile floor. Early one morning, at about 1:00, we heard loud noises followed by vicious barking, an agonizing cry, and the sound of long toenails running in place on the tile floor—all of which ended with a huge *thump*. This repeated over and over for about forty-five seconds. Thinking we had an intruder, we grabbed our gun and frantically ran down the hall.

As we passed my mom's room, she excitedly asked me, "What the hell is going on, Pam?"

We ignored her, continuing down the hall toward the noise, but when we arrived, there was complete silence. All noise had stopped. There was Dexter violently shaking with a bewildered gaze on his face. He then took off down the hall into our master bedroom, only stopping once to turn around and peek to see if anything horrible was following him.

There was no sign of anyone.

For months afterwards, he made sure to sleep right up against us and would even refuse to negotiate going into the hallway until he had stuck his handsome head around the corner to make sure the coast was clear. His personality had changed drastically, and I needed to find out exactly what had made him so fearful and skittish.

Case in point: there would be times my husband and I would be watching TV and all of a sudden, Dexter would start running around the room frantically until he hid his head behind a table or another piece of furniture. His head would be hidden, but the rest of his body would be hanging totally out in plain sight. I guess in his mind if he couldn't see it, it couldn't see him. Whatever it was, whatever was really happening, was scaring the life out of him. Something terrible had traumatized and hurt our dog. This was war!

We assumed with good reason that this was Howard's handiwork. After all, wasn't he the only ghost we'd seen to date besides the little girl? Who else could it be? A friend of ours suggested that we have a medium come in and try to pass Howard on to his final resting place. Arriving with arms loaded with sage and holy water, she blessed the house and voiced an earnest desire for the return of peace and tranquility to our home. Afterwards, she assured us that, yes, Howard had "passed." Upon hearing this I, for one, could not stop doing the happy dance over and over again. I soon realized that was a little premature.

That very night, things started to escalate.

I heard a sudden noise coming from the master bathroom. I thought that one of our dogs must be in there. I was wrong. There was no one I could see there. I texted my sister in the guest bedroom down the hall and told her something bad is here!

She said, "I will meet you in the kitchen right now!"

As I started down the hall, something very, very tall came up behind me with a presence so strong that I could easily feel its energy. Running as fast as I could down the hall to meet my sister, he kept pace with me, breathing down my neck and frequently pulling on the back of my hair. Rushing up to my sister, I told her that Howard must be extremely angry.

She said "No, Pam, this is not Howard!" Whatever it was, was much, much darker and stronger than Howard.

Seeing the terror on my face, my sister put her back to mine, faced this entity, and proceeded to tell it to back off. After a period of time, we eventually went to our separate beds, both sleeping with one eye open that night.

The next morning, my sister and I sat down for our morning coffee, and she wanted to talk about what had happened the previous night. She was very concerned about how petrified I was and expressed that this entity was feeding off of my fear.

She said, "Pam, you should call on God's protection and not let this thing intimidate you!"

Let me just say, this is easier said than done!

I sat down and started to reflect on how much I loved our vacation house—despite the paranormal happenings. We'd invested thousands of dollars to make it just the way we wanted it to be, and before all this started, we felt very much at home there.

During happier times, I would arrive at the house a few days before my husband did in order to get things ready, and he would follow after he got off work on Thursdays. That soon stopped happening since there was simply no way at this point that I was going to go there all by my lonesome.

One night at about 12:30, when I was asleep, lying on my side and facing the wall, I felt like something was watching me. I got the courage up to open my eyes and saw an orb at eye level, only about eight inches from my face. It was extremely bright and totally round. I jerked myself upright, and it suddenly disappeared. The next night it was very hot, so I was lying directly on my back with no covers over me. At about the same time—12:30 a.m.—some strange force grabbed me by the shoulders and roughly picked me up and threw me back down. This thing, this force, did this six more times, and with each time I moved closer to the headboard, eventually hitting my head against it. The force was holding my arm down on the side of my husband, virtually locking it against my body so I could not reach out for help. It took me lifting my other arm, fighting with all my might so I could knock over the lamp on my nightstand, which finally woke my husband up.

He yelled, "What the hell is going on?"

I could not see anyone but felt I had fallen under full demonic attack!

I was so terrified; I just lay there and trembled the rest of the night. All I could think was, "Was this Howard?" Why was he so angry with me? Or could this be the evil spirit my sister said was stronger than strong and darker than dark? I was starting to feel beyond desperate. I didn't know what was happening to me and didn't have a single clue as to what to do about it. At my wit's end, I shared my experience with a co-worker friend. She suggested a house clearing. As it turned out, she and her girlfriend were experienced in this area.

So, we scheduled a date! My husband and I went up the day before to get things ready. And then our plans went amiss.

They were scheduled to arrive the next day, but it seemed that something or someone was trying to thwart their plans. After numerous missed turns and wrong directions, they finally made it safely to the cottage.

Part of the ceremony consisted of writing up a contract and then burning it outside the house. That step, however, did not go over too well with Howard. You see, he was a retired fire chief. As far as fire was concerned, he just wasn't having it. Every time they set fire to the contract, something blew it out. On the fourth try, in fact, that something slapped the arm of the woman who was trying to light the contract on fire. Eventually, Howard gave up and they were able to light the fire needed.

Interestingly enough, my two ghostbuster friends picked up on several things. First of all, they got shivers when entering the master bathroom. One of them made the comment this could be a portal. It made sense to me because of all the noise that originated from that bathroom. There were several nights that I was awakened by a long, loud crackling sound. It sounded as if someone was crunching up pieces of plastic mylar paper.

The other lady managed to pick up on the energy of an inebriated Native American chief with an Indian coyote headdress on his head. That was yet another WTH moment for me as I remembered seeing him coming down the hall toward our bedroom one night while I was lying awake in bed. He was so tall I thought I saw him hit the chandelier with his headdress. This had happened a couple months earlier, and at the time, I thought I was seeing things with my post-surgery eyes again. His shoulders were so wide they almost filled the entire hallway. He was naked from the waist up with a deerskin loincloth from the waist down to his high thighs. His feet and calves were encased in moccasin boots. He had several chunky necklaces around his neck that I could not make out. There was some type of black marking on his face, but I have to admit, most of my attention was focused on the coyote on the top of his head. He defined the word menacing. At last, though, the dots were beginning to connect, and things were beginning to make sense. All this time I'd been blaming Howard! The ladies put some of my fears and suspicions to rest. They let me know that not only was old Howard innocent of all wrongdoing but that, in fact, he'd been doing his best all along to protect us.

But now I was aware of a new intruder.

Continuing with my new understanding, I thought about what my dog had gone through, sleeping by the front door and seeing a large Indian chief with a coyote on his head. No wonder Dexter freaked out! Just thinking about it was freaking me out. Fortunately, I was able finally to figure out what was behind that much-repeated thumping sound. It was the sound of that man literally pushing my dog down on the floor, again and again and again. After topping off their spirit-cleansing work with a salt ceremony, the ladies suggested that all these events were due to the actions of a drunken Indian chief with a coyote on his head. I thought this could not be happening.

After talking with others who are familiar with the Native American culture, it was strongly recommended that we ask a shaman to address the situation. I was told they would know exactly how to pass a Native American spirit to the other side, so it would be a win-win for us all.

A dear friend whom I had known for years was very knowledgeable in this and was willing to take on the task. We scheduled a time to meet by phone when I was up at our vacation home to give it a try. I must admit I was very skeptical but didn't want to hurt her feelings. I merged my sister and her on a call so we could all be united in prayer together. After much preparation, we were ready to guide this Native American spirit to the other side. We felt he was either going to go willingly, or the angels were going to drag him across.

"He was so tall I thought I saw him hit the chandelier with his headdress..."

Praying to God and calling on as many angels as we could by faith, we believed this strong warrior spirit was finally at peace and no longer living with us at our vacation home.

I have to admit I had so much faith during the ceremony, but when darkness fell that night—I just waited. For several nights I lived in fear, waiting for him to be so angry at me that he'd pick me up and literally throw me out the window! Thank God that night never came!

That was many years ago, and through the grace of God, there have been no further occurrences.

And That's
Our Mom
For You!

✝

Pam Mandel

Pam and Karen with our Mom in September 2017

Please indulge me for a few minutes and kindly allow me the pleasure of talking about our mom. My sister and I are both in our sixties and have had more than enough time to learn that no one in your life will ever love you as much as your mother. After all, aren't all moms special? Ours was exceptionally so—full of life and positivity no matter what state her health was in. She lived on less than half a functioning heart for decades and, during that time, made the most out of whatever energy was available to her. It's almost a cliché now, but we will say it anyway—everyone loved her. After all, how many people do you know had the same best friend for seventy-six years! Loving, kind, giving, tolerant-to-a-fault, tenacious, and so stubborn that you had to laugh, no matter what, she was loyal to her family.

And she was our best friend, so much so that she, my sister, and I were referred to as the three amigos. We just loved to be together, often taking "just us girls" vacations together and laughing so hard one time that I actually passed out briefly! There was another dimension to all this besides all those moments of rip-roaring levity. She kept educating us in the finer points (and some of the not so fine ones) of life, right up to the minute she passed. When she died, she did so with dignity, keeping things in those last moments as calm and as low-key as possible.

Our Parents at Pam and Michael's Wedding on February 14, 1998

My parents lived with my sister and her husband for eight years. After our dad passed away in 2008, she continued to live with them, visiting me for several weeks at a time every few months. Because of my sister's worsening health, however, in 2014 she permanently joined my husband and me in our Bay Area home just outside San Francisco. She was a strong and wonderful woman and brought much joy to our home. Living with only thirty-two percent of coronary capacity for the past nineteen years did not stop her from enjoying life and living it to the fullest. Her love of gardening kept her busy for hours on end, and she was pretty darned good at it. Whereas she and my sister Karen were two peas in a pod when it came to their love of the soil.

But then it happened.

On Sunday, October 1, 2017, while driving home with me from our vacation house, Mom began to complain that the band around her bra was crushing her chest. I pulled over to the side of the road to see if we could relieve the pressure by loosening it (the bra). After some time had gone by, she said it was getting better but that she still felt a bit off. Since she'd just been exposed to the waning stages of my son's bout of the flu, I suggested that we give it some time, and if she felt the same the next day, we'd have it checked out. Her breathing had gotten worse by the next day, so I called for an ambulance to take her to the ER. After several tests, it was determined that she had suffered a major heart attack on that ride back from our vacation house, and her heart was now working at less than seven percent capacity. She was immediately admitted to the hospital and placed in "comfy care." I lost no time in calling my sister, who lives in Las Vegas, and imploring her to hurry to join us since Mom couldn't possibly hold on much longer.

After spending several days on a morphine drip, she started to go downhill rapidly. We made sure at this point that she was never alone. Surrounded by loved ones, she had someone there twenty-four hours a day. When evening came, I made a bed on the couch in her room so that I could continue to keep her company. Sometime on the fourth day of being on the morphine drip, I could hear her moaning. I called for the nurse, who wanted to give her more morphine to alleviate the pain. I tried to find out what was wrong by asking her to squeeze my hand if she was in pain. She didn't squeeze it. When I asked her to squeeze my hand if she was not in pain, she squeezed it with whatever strength she had left. When I moved my head as close to her mouth as possible to see if I could hear her tell me what was wrong, she vomited all over me. Her state of extreme nausea convinced her attending nurse to do some investigating. It turns out that they had given her too much morphine, so they lightened up her dosage. Although she had vomited all over my hair and all down the front of my clothing, I was hesitant to leave her to go home and change since I knew full well that her time to pass was so near. The nurse gave me a hospital gown to change into. After a couple hours, my sister and I decided to go home and return as soon as possible. I called my husband to come from work to keep Mom company while we went home for a quick shower.

After a lightning-quick shower, I was ready to return to the hospital as soon as possible, knowing that her days were numbered and not wanting to miss a single moment of whatever time she had left. As I was walking out of my bedroom with towels to be deposited in the laundry room hamper, I saw her, standing by her baby grand piano and sporting the biggest smile I'd ever seen on that often-smiling face. I was shocked! I yelled for Karen, "Come quick! Mom is here!" I kept repeating it: "Mom is here!" By the time Karen came from her bedroom to the living room, Mom had disappeared. It only took a few seconds for it to dawn on me.

She had passed. Mom was gone. No sooner had I begun to wonder out loud why my husband hadn't called us to let us know she had passed than we heard the phone ring. I picked up the handset, knowing full well that I was going to hear what we have been dreading all this time.

Seeing that the Caller ID was his, I greeted him with, "I already know, she's gone."

Michael said, "I am so sorry, hon. It just happened. They want to know if you would like to come and sit by her."

I immediately said, "Why? She is not there anymore; she was here within seconds after she passed. She is happy, out of pain, and she can breathe again on her own!"

Knowing that she was no longer in her body at the hospital, there was no reason to go and sit by her.

I can't express how much we miss our mom. After our Dad passed away, Karen and I, for the last nine years of her life, made sure all her needs were met. My sister use to tell me that I treated Mom like my very own live Barbie doll, always making sure her purse and shoes matched, along with having her hair and nails done on a regular basis. I guess my sister was right and, boy, did I enjoy it. But really, she was the almost perfect mother—even better than June Cleaver, in spite of the fact that we never saw her doing any house cleaning in pearls and high heels (LOL)!

Over the next few months, I saw Mom on two occasions. The first time, she appeared in the form of a white mist at the entrance to the laundry room. One moment she was there, and in the next moment she was gone. Poof . . . vanished within a few seconds. The second time was more interesting; so much so, in fact, that I don't think I'll ever forget it. I was in her room, changing her bedding after having entertained overnight guests. I was standing on the opposite side of the bed from the doorway, facing the door, when I saw her walking down the hall in her favorite leopard pajamas. Although her hair was totally gray when she passed away, it was now light brown and highlighted with blonde (OMG, do they have beauticians in Heaven?). As she passed the doorway to her room, she waved at me and smiled from ear to ear, all the while moving at a steady pace without missing a beat. I mention this last fact because, you see, before she passed, she could barely put one foot in front of the other even with the help of a walker. I could hardly believe it and was delighted to see how happy she was!

About four months after she passed, my husband and I were in bed one night when he said to me, "Who is that talking out in the family room?"

Then all of a sudden, Alexa said, "Here is your selection: 'You Raise Me Up' by Josh Groban."

Again, we could scarcely believe it—it was my Mom's favorite song. I asked my husband if the voice he heard before Alexa spoke was a woman's voice or a man's? He said it was a woman's voice. Could it have been Mom? A few weeks later, my son and I were sitting in our living room and laughing over something my mom had done a couple years before when the light on the end table began to blink off and on. Amazingly, it just so happened that it began to do so just when we had finished laughing. The lamp had never done that before and has never done it since. Could it have been my mom listening to us talk about her and trying to get her two cents in?

One Saturday afternoon at the beginning of December 2018, my husband and I were working together on getting our Christmas lights in place on the roof. I'd gone into my walk-in closet to change my shoes so I could go outside to help him by holding the ladder. When I kicked off my slippers, one went to the left side of the closet while the other went to the right side. After a couple hours I came back in to take off my work shoes and put my slippers back on. The slippers were not where I had left them, so I looked on the bottom rack, under my clothing, and found them arranged neatly, side by side, on top of my mom's purse. At first, I was stumped, to say the least, since I had been unable to bring myself even to touch my mom's purse since she had passed away. It was something she always carried with her, so I had put it in the corner of the closet for safekeeping. My next thought calmed me immeasurably. It was simply this: Mom was letting me know she is with us in spirit at all times. I immediately felt her love and started to cry.

My sister has been sick and in severe pain for many years, collecting diagnoses from a whole bunch of doctors. Among the professional opinions rendered were fibromyalgia, diabetes, high blood pressure, and costochondritis, etc., but no real explanation for the degree of pain she was in 24/7. That pain was so bad at this point that she couldn't even get out of bed in the morning. One day while I was having a reading on the phone by Sara Lopez, from Arizona, our mom came through and told her that Karen is very ill with Hashimoto's. My first thought upon hearing that was, "How the hell do I spell that?" So, I looked it up on the Internet, hoping for the best. I found out that it is an autoimmune thyroid disease that causes all sorts of issues with the body, including severe stiffness in the joints as well as aches and pains everywhere. Neither of us had ever heard of it before.

I asked Karen to make a doctor's appointment and get tested. Of course, she could hardly tell her doctor that our dead mother had diagnosed her! I mean, can you imagine? So instead, she told her doctor that a physician friend of hers from California, after hearing Karen describe the symptoms, said that it sounds like she does indeed have Hashimoto's disease. Anyway, long story short, after a simple blood test was taken, it was discovered that—lo and behold—she was suffering from Hashimoto's!

My sister came to visit us, and she always stayed in Mom's old room. As always, Mom was on her mind throughout her stay. One night at around 10:00, she went out to the backyard to have the last cigarette of the day. It was a beautiful night, and she was enjoying the peace and quiet when, all of a sudden, as she later told me, she could hear our mom's voice saying in a tone that was as clear as a bell: "Karen, Karen."

Karen answered with, "I hear you, Mom."

Mom proceeded to tell her that she needed to get a colonoscopy done ASAP, saying it with such urgency that Karen's answer was short, sweet, and to the point: "Okay!" Then Mom went on to tell her that although her cigarette smoking had not caused her body any obvious harm yet, it soon would. Mom then added that Karen needed to quit ASAP! Again, it was said with such urgency that she promised Mom that she would do so immediately. Mom was about to say something else, but Karen was so overwhelmed by their conversation that she interrupted Mom, asking her if she had any good news, such as "Honey, did you know that you´re going to live to be ninety?" or some such.

Mom replied, "Yes, I love you," and then she did something that Karen will never forget. She placed her hand just above my sister's knee. As the heat from Mom's hand coursed through my sister's being, she felt the incredible spiritual love that Mom had for her. At that moment, all was well in the world again for Karen, well and good like it hadn't been since our mother had passed.

To this day, I seriously wonder if we can survive without our talks with Mom (yes, she joins in our conversations at times). Through it all, our mother has helped us to see the afterlife very, very differently.

And that's our Mom for you!

Mom on Christmas of 2016

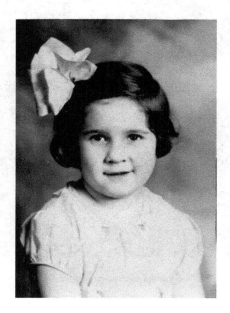

Mom in 1939

Mom in 2015

Ghost Dogs

✝

Pam Mandel
& Karen Pena

2008 – 2020

What began as a mutual-services contract between two very different species became something much more like love. None of that makes a lick of sense, but it doesn't have to. Love rarely touches the reasoning parts of the brain. It touches the dreamy parts, the devoted parts—it touches the parts we sometimes call the heart. For many thousands of years, it's there that our dogs have lived.
–Time magazine

Years ago, a deacon in our church told us that animals—dogs included—do not go to heaven. We struggled with that for years, trying to understand how those loving creatures that made our lives so much better could be left behind and excluded from that place that so many humans aspire to as a final destination.

Here are a few of our experiences that have led us seriously to question the good deacon's claim.

KAREN'S STORY

My sister and I absolutely adore dogs! We have always had them in our lives, starting from a very early age. We are now in our early sixties and have been blessed with many dogs over the decades. The first spirit dog I was aware of was my beautiful sweet collie Seanie. I can't say enough about how smart, kind, and compassionate she was—nothing less than a mother to all dogs. She was the best dog I had ever had, and my husband and I adored her completely. Her official AKC name was "Royal Joy of Heart," a name that she lived up to in every possible way.

When she was eight years old, she had a back injury and could not move. The vet wanted to put her down. We said no, and instead, we put her on medication and took her home. Driven by desperation, we took her into our hot tub every day and just let the jets of hot water roll over her and soothe her pain-wracked body. We had to carry her everywhere at first, but little by little she regained her ability to move until she was finally able to walk again.

We'd had our miracle! She lived another six years, years filled with happiness and love for all of us. I always knew that Seanie would let me know when it was time for her to pass (yep, she was that smart). One morning, as soon as I woke up, I saw that something was terribly wrong with her. She had had a stroke during the night. I started to panic. First, I called my husband, and then our veterinarian. Then I put the phone down and just looked at her. It hit me, and I knew. That look in her eyes, that sad, sad pleading look told me very clearly what she was trying to say.

It was her time.

Although all this happened years ago, as I am writing this, I am crying my eyes out. That's how much I loved that dog. When she was gone, I could not be consoled by anything or anyone. It is not an exaggeration to say that I was utterly devastated. I was beyond sad, beyond comforting, crying 24/7 over the loss of my best friend. My husband, torn up by what was going on inside me, took me on a vacation to take my mind off of our loss. It was a noble gesture but one that, unfortunately, failed completely. In fact, we ended up coming home early because I just couldn't respond to this attempt to ease my return to the land of the living.

This went on for a month or more.

Then one morning I woke up, sat up in bed, and looked

over to where Seanie had always slept. There she was, lying there in her usual spot and looking up at me with a big smile on her face (yes, dogs do smile)! After what seemed like an eternity had gone by, I was finally able to take my eyes off her. Before I did, however, I noticed that she was somehow different from the way she was when she passed. Then I realized what that difference was! She was young, beautiful, and healthy again, just like she was when she was around three years old. My heart soared, and a strange but abiding peace settled over me. Then she slowly disappeared, evaporating along with all my sadness.

Years have passed since then. I still see her now and then, mostly when I need to.

I have lost two more dogs since losing Seanie. I have also seen their spirits after they passed, playing and running, young again and full of life. Sometimes they are even running with Seanie.

"If there are no dogs in Heaven, then when I die I want to go where they went."
—Will Rogers

PAM'S STORY

Molly was our pomapoo dog, which means she was half Poodle and half Pomeranian. Thinking back on this little bundle of life, who became one of the family in 2006, all I can say is talk about a dog with a mind of her own! Molly did whatever she wanted to and far be it from anyone to tell her different. Case in point: how many dogs have you seen who could climb straight up a wall with no problem? Having rescued her from being put down because of her bad back legs at age six months, we knew that she would always be fragile. This was never so true as it was during the last few years of her blessed existence on this earth.

One of our other dogs, Tucker, was a little seven-pound poodle that we'd inherited from our son. He'd become quite close to Molly over the past couple of years of her life, and the two became inseparable best buds. They slept together in the same doggie bed, groomed each other incessantly, and followed each other just about everywhere.

Over two years, it became apparent that the time had come for us to do what we had been dreading for some time. It was time to put Molly down. She wouldn't eat anymore, she had trouble defecating, and her energy level was dangerously low.

You could tell she was in great pain just trying to get out of her furry bed. So, at the advice of our vet, we decided not to wait any longer. We have always had a special vet come to our house when a dog of ours had reached the end of his or her life. We feel it is so much better both for them and for us as it serves greatly to reduce the stress level for all.

On the day the vet came to the house, we made sure that our eighty-pound Goldendoodle was out of the way and in the car. He is so rambunctious that he would have created nothing but chaos during this sensitive time. Our vet is such a dog-lover that little Tucker ran right over to her and just sat on her lap, enjoying every moment of the ever-so-affectionate stroking he got from her. We then put Molly on the floor in her bed while I held Tucker in my lap on the couch.

My husband was busy showing Molly great big heaps of love while the vet administered the necessary medication. After a few minutes, she checked Molly's vital signs and pronounced her dead. I put Tucker down on the floor, knowing he wanted to jump right back on our vet's lap for more of that stroking time. While running toward the vet, however, he came to an abrupt stop!

All of a sudden, he lay down with his paws outstretched. He held that position for about a minute, staying very still and staring at his buddy Molly all the while. All of a sudden, he jumped up and circled around a nearby chair as if he were heading her off in another direction (maybe to the kitchen). His tail wagging, he looked as though he were happily chasing her. Did he see her leave her body and head that way? Was she suddenly hungry after not eating for days? We honestly didn't know. But we do know that Tucker has always been able to perceive and see things that we might not, and we are convinced that he saw Molly on the run and chased after her. Amazingly, our vet said she has seen similar situations many times over the years.

Several years before we lost Molly, her best friend Toodles, a small terrier/poodle mix, passed away. Boy, did this little guy love bones! We would give all three dogs a bone and within no time, Toodles had them all in his mouth. With such a small mouth, we were amazed that he could maneuver them so they all fit. A couple weeks after Toodles passed away, one night I was working in my office when I heard a noise. I stopped typing and just sat there and listened for a moment. I thought it sounded just like a dog chewing a bone. All of a sudden, something began to rub up against my legs. I then put two and two together and realized that was Toodles favorite place to lie, right by my feet under my desk. I thought, even in the afterlife, he is stealing all the other doggies' bones!

My husband and I have also noticed many other times when we feel something brushing up against us, at which point we look down and invariably see that nothing is there. It is as if one of our beloved past pets is visiting us to say hello. On many occasions, I have witnessed a flash in the form of an animal running across the living room or bedroom, only to disappear in the blink of an eye. One time we both could hear a dog tag from a collar hitting the water bowl in our house. Was it just an illusion, or was it the ghost of one of them? I would like to think that pets live on after death and even come around occasionally to reassure us they are okay and are waiting for us to join them someday!

OUR HOPE

Our hope is that these stories can bring comfort to those of us who have lost an animal we loved. Even if you don't see them after they've departed this planet, just know that they are in Heaven. For our part, we look forward to rejoining all of our beloved fur babies eventually.

"Until one has loved an animal a part of one's soul remains unawakened."
- Anatole France

9

A Kick
From The Grave

✝

Pam Mandel

2018

I never met my husband's father.

When he passed away over fifty years ago, my husband Michael was barely eighteen. Most of what I knew of his dad came from discussions around family get-togethers with my husband, his siblings, and his mom. Of the precious few photos that my husband was able to show me, my hands-down favorite was his mom and dad's wedding photo. They were a good-looking couple, and I never got tired of seeing them beaming at the photographer on their wedding day.

Michael's Mom and Dad Celebrating their Wedding Day
on August 20, 1948

When Michael and his siblings shared stories about their dad, they gave the strong impression that he was a strict, no-nonsense military father who believed in the use of punishment as a correctional tool and a man who showed very little love in an open and physical manner. In short, he was, above all, a man who fit the profile of a typical 1950s dad.

When my husband's mom was passing, he immediately flew to spend her last moments with her, along with his brother and his wife. When he got all settled in, he FaceTimed me from her bedside during her final hours so I could say my good-byes to her. Although she wasn't conscious, I still wanted to let her know that I loved her and would miss her greatly.

Funny thing, though, as I was watching them on my computer screen, I noticed a man in the corner of her room who closely resembled my husband's father. He was wearing blue pants, dark shoes, white socks, and a thick white, wrinkle-free t-shirt with a pack of cigs rolled up in his sleeve. He looked to be in his mid-thirties and he just stood there, seemingly watching the activity in the room. There were also three ladies who stood out in the FaceTime video. I recognized one of them as being my husband's mom's sister, who had passed away a few months before, but regarding the other two I could only draw a blank.

Later that day, his mom passed.

The next day, my sister and I went to a local bagel shop. Seated at an outdoor patio table, I was telling her about what I'd seen in the room and mentioned that I thought the man in the corner looked a lot like the photos I had seen of my husband's father. At the precise moment when I mentioned him to my sister, something kicked my chair four times, four times and with so much force that the chair actually moved with each kick. I quickly looked down to see what was happening. For an instant I thought that maybe one of the legs of the chair had slipped into a crack in the cement. My sister said she thought she'd seen something that was black, blue, and white—maybe a bird? Looking around I didn't see anything, not even a bird, and on second thought I seriously had to doubt a bird's ability (maybe except for an eagle or condor) to move a chair.

I continued my story. When I got to the part where I confessed that I thought it was my husband's father I had seen in the bedroom, it happened again—the same four hard kicks. I quickly got up and looked around, and again I saw nothing. This time my sister, who was sitting across from me, chimed in with some information that made this already freaked-out situation even freakier:

"You are not going to believe this, but it actually looked like a foot—a single foot!"

Not believing her for a second, I sat back down, thinking I was never going to be able to finish my story, but I tried again and continued with my story. When I mentioned the mysterious intruder's name again, OMG, four hard kicks again and that is when I saw the foot in question. I was ready for it that time! A single foot that was encased in a black shoe and white sock, and above it was the cuff of a blue pant leg.

I then said, "OMG, are you trying to let me know it was you?" "Dad, I never met you, but I know now that it was you in that room waiting to take your wife to the other side."

After letting him know that everyone really appreciated him being there, the kicking came to an end. Apparently, it was very important for him to let us know that he was there for her during this time. I finally was able to complete my story with my sister.

As I reflected back, I couldn't help but wonder why four kicks. Could it be because they had four children together?

As far as I knew, before I saw him in the room with his dying wife, Michael's dad had never reached out to me. That's why I was surprised when, out of the blue, I was having this interaction with him. I could only deduce from our strange history that, for some reason, it was of the utmost importance to him that his kids know that he really loved them and was sorry for many, many things. Most of all he wanted them to understand that his emphasis on the material side of things—taking care of the bills, putting food on the table, and leaving them with a paid-off house—was motivated by his love for them. I got the feeling that it was only after his passing, unfortunately, when he realized his kids also needed hugs as much as they needed the household's bills paid on time.

A few weeks later, Michael's dad again reached out to me from beyond, letting me know that he wanted me to tell Michael's brother that he loved him. When I suggested that it was something that he himself should take care of, he agreed. I called Michael's brother and told him to be prepared for a visit from his dad. Two days later, I received a call from his brother's wife telling me that an invisible presence had squeezed her husband's ankle in a loving way. Having received that heads-up from me about an impending visitation, Michael's brother knew it was his dad.

My fervent wish is that their dad gets some kind of closure.

Michael with his Dad and Brother in 1962

Touched by
Our Angels
✝
Pam Mandel
& Karen Pena

PAM MANDEL'S STORY - 1980

When I was in my early twenties, I bought a new, all-white— inside and out—1979 VW convertible. Boy, was it super cute and so girly-looking. I just loved driving it around town with the top down, letting my long hair just blow in the wind. One afternoon, not too long after I bought it, I was driving down the freeway taking off the ramp to make a left onto the main road. When I started to make my left, I noticed a huge semi-truck traveling down the road so fast that it was going to come barreling through the light right towards me as I was making a left turn. There was not enough time to think, much less react to what was about to happen. I just knew this was it! I was going to die! As the truck came rushing straight at me, I screamed "Jesus, help me!"

The next moment I remember was sitting in my car in a parking lot, right next to the road. I could not believe it! What had just happened? My vehicle was properly positioned, perfectly spaced evenly, in a valid parking space with the engine turned off. I had no idea how or what had just happened (not to mention why) , but somehow my car, with me sitting safe and sound in it, had been whisked out of harm's way. I just sat there and began to cry and cry, with tears and makeup running down my face! At that moment, it is really hard to express, but the feeling of God taking the time to send his divine intervention for me—to save my life-totally overwhelmed me, and it took my belief in God to a whole new level. There was no one out there who could convince me that God didn't exist or that I was ever alone!

It helped me to realize that, as much as an almost unbearable degree of torment can exist in a supernatural dimension, there's also the protective love that God shows His children. If they had traffic cameras back then and it had captured footage of the collision, I wonder what it would have recorded. Did the person driving that truck have a similar experience? These are questions that I will never know the answers to until I pass to the other side.

KAREN PENA'S STORIES

First Angel - 1981

I was twenty-three years old the first time I saw an angel.

I woke up suddenly and glanced at the clock on my night table. The digital display read 2:12 a.m. It turned out that I had acquired a bedmate while I was asleep—a supernatural being enveloped in an aura of golden light was at the foot of my bed holding my dog in its arms. I immediately felt such overwhelming feelings of love, compassion, and everything that was good in this universe radiating itself out of this wonderful creature.

I will try my best to describe this extraordinary being that was neither male nor female (the first thing that I noticed). It was very tall and wore a long, light blue shift covered by a thick white flowing robe secured at the waist with a white belt. Its longish face was graced with an aquiline nose and golden hair that flowed past its shoulders and was parted down the middle, and its piercing blue-gold eyes alternated their glance between the dog it held so lovingly and me.

Undefinable by gender, this heavenly being was a font of love, peace, and goodness. I stared at this majestic creation for a long time, happily soaking up the love, peace, and goodness that flowed from its core. Then, as suddenly as it had introduced itself into my life, it disappeared, letting my dog get back to his snoring. To this day, I have no idea why God allowed me to see this, but I do know that over the years I have re-lived this experience again and again when I needed to reactivate my faith in the eternal.

Second Angel - 1983

The second time I saw an angel was a few years later.

I was driving through Sunol Canyon at 6:00 in the morning during a rainstorm. I was in my sports car and driving way too fast-and-crazy for the prevailing road and weather conditions. That is when my vehicle spun out of control on a dangerous curve with a mountain on one side and a cliff on the other. When the car bounced off the mountainside and started toward the cliff, I screamed out one word at the top of my lungs: "Jesus!"

And then it was there.

Again.

I recognized that supernatural golden glow immediately and just sat behind the wheel with eyes closed while the angel picked up my car and put it back down on the right side of the road—perfectly still and pointed in the right direction. I sat in the motionless vehicle, alive and unscathed, and as a feeling that was equal parts gratitude and bliss made its way from my head to my toes and back again, I was eventually left with the cold and sober realization that

I had been supernaturally saved from certain death. Was it the same angel I had seen before? Thank you, Jesus.

Third Angel - 1996

My third angelic encounter took place when I was thirty-eight years old and revolved around the presence of (what I can only describe as) an angel in my house in San Jose. At the time, I had a parrot named Sophia that loved to talk to anyone. When not entertaining visitors with "Hello" or "I love you" she often regaled them with whistled passages from the score of *Phantom of the Opera*. At night I would cover her cage, which was located in the family room on the first floor of the house, with a huge yellow blanket so she could sleep peacefully.

Late at night, when the uninvited spiritual activity in my bedroom started to become overwhelming, I would often hear Sophia talking downstairs. Hearing her say "Hello" over and over again clued me in to the fact that someone was near her cage. Peering over the balcony to see what was going on downstairs, all I could make out was that unmistakable supernatural gold glow emanating from Sophie's cage and filling the entire ground floor of the house. And just like they had on those other occasions on which I'd encountered that angelic presence, waves of love and peace came rushing over me. I asked myself on those many nights when that divine protection was there for my husband, my kids, my animals, and myself—was it the same angel?

Fourth Angel - 2016

My sister was having her vacation house spiritually cleansed by a medium. At the time we were trying to pass the former owner of the property, who had passed away in the house, onto the next level of being.

Pam and I had spent hours at prayer before the cleansing. Shortly after her arrival on the day of the ritual, the medium and Pam were going over some details in the kitchen when I decided to go out onto the deck to get some fresh air. What I saw was amazing, so amazing that just thinking about it while I'm putting it all down on paper gives me chills all over my body. Right there in front of me, standing in a row and making eye contact with me, were twelve angels linked together, bathed in an exquisite golden light. I was filled with awe before this indescribably beautiful scene. Once again, that supernatural peace came over me, and I just knew that they had been sent there to aid and support us.

I closed my eyes, took a deep breath, slowly exhaled, and thought to myself, "God is great."

Room 312

✠

Pam Mandel

May 2017

Throughout its history, Key West and the Keys in general have held a bit of the frontier. Outlaw mystique, adventurers, castaways, smugglers, runaways, and renegade souls of various stripes have always been and still are attracted to the area. And a significant part the Keys' regional lore is the many tales of the exploits

THE HAUNTINGS OF TWO SISTERS

of the pirates of the Florida Keys and the Caribbean waters beyond.

Some decisions in life are simple and straightforward: where to have lunch, where to get your oil changed, whether to order a la carte or not, which movie to watch on Netflix, etc. It's safe to say that none of these decisions, like the innumerable ones we make in the course of a typical day, is expected to be a life-changing event.

The decision my husband and I made to visit Key West during May of 2017 was not one of those decisions.

Our original reason for our Sunshine State vacation was to catch a sailfish or two in the waters off West Palm Beach. Once there, we felt that we more than made up for our lack of luck in that department with a heck of a catch—right up to the legal limit—of mahi-mahi instead. Our lovely day on the blue waters of South Florida nearing its end, I think my husband and I knew that we were still not quite ready to say goodbye to the land of coconut palms and piña coladas.

Pam Fishing off the Florida Coast in May 2017

After cleaning our fish and preparing a few choice specimens for that evening's dinner, Michael and I gave each other that look—the look of recognition of yet another good thing coming to an end, the look you might see on the faces of two kids who just heard the "thirty minutes until closing" warning over the P.A. system at Disney World telling them that the best day of their young lives was about to come to an end.

And then we saw it.

Michael had just packed the last fish in our cooler and was about to start carrying our gear to the dock. All of a sudden, I thought to remind him to look down and make sure that he hadn't forgotten anything. He looked down at the sheet of newspaper on which he had placed his paraphernalia. He stopped moving, apparently transfixed by something he saw. He asked me to come over and take a look. It turned out that his attention had been focused on a newspaper advertisement for a hotel on Key West, and in the ad, there was mention of that island town's colorful past in the Great Age of Piracy!

We looked at each other lovingly, giggling like a couple of kids at our good fortune. You see, we'd already heard about Key West's many charms and couldn't quite put the thought of visiting this dreamy island destination out of our minds. Already convinced that this gem of a town was out of this world, what we didn't know was that our visit would involve a whole bunch of experiences that would indeed be, in the most literal sense, exactly that: out of this world.

Key West is a tropical fantasy of palm-kissed beaches, pastel painted homes, and always-smiling natives, or "Conchs." We could have flown the 165 miles from Miami but decided on a leisurely drive on the scenic causeway in our convertible rental car. The place advertised in the newspaper was nothing less than a five-star remodeled historical hotel in the center of town, a location that put us right in the center of the action. We wasted no time in making a reservation. Later that day we found ourselves standing in front of Key West's southernmost point buoy marker, the one that told us that we were a few feet away from the southernmost point in the United States. Surrounded by breathtakingly blue water and some of the best beaches in the world, we were delighted to breathe in the full and vibrant history of this corner of paradise!

Michael and Pam at Key West, FL in May 2017

What could go wrong?

Exactly, what could go wrong! We spent that evening of our romantic adventure in Key West with a beautiful dinner cruise on crystal blue waters, taking in the sights while savoring the sea breeze that gently brushed our faces. Afterwards, we walked the downtown streets, enjoying the many unique artists and musicians. And yes, we enjoyed our very first taste of Key lime pie, becoming instant fans of the local delicacy!

After a full day of driving, shopping, good food, and lots of walking, we were ready to check into our hotel for a quiet and restful evening. Our room had two double beds with a TV set directly in front of one of them. Although my husband was very tired and wanted to go right to sleep, I still had some awake time in me and decided to turn on the television. He suggested that we sleep in separate beds so he could get some sleep while I watched TV. I thought this was a great idea.

And then it happened.

I eventually fell asleep on my side with my back to my husband. At approximately 1:00 a.m., I was awakened with the sensation of fingertips lightly caressing my hip. "Hmmm, I thought, hubby must have woken up feeling a bit lonely! A few seconds later, however, I could hear him snoring. OMG, I thought, what the hell?" I just lay there and didn't move, waiting to see what was going to happen next. A few minutes later I saw the bed covers creeping down toward the bottom of the bed and eventually falling off the bed to the floor. By now I was thinking a lot worse than "OMG" and "What the hell?"

I remained completely still, desperately trying to figure out what was happening. About a minute after the bed covers fell to the floor, I could see knee imprints advancing towards me from the other side of the bed. That is when I totally lost it and jumped out of bed, screaming over and over again "SOMETHING IS IN THE ROOM!"

My husband jumped up, ready to fight, saying "WHERE? WHERE?"

I said, "I don't know, but believe me, it is here"!

The look he gave me was priceless! I told him at least three times what had happened, and I feel he just didn't get it because I guess he thought I must have been having a bad dream.

Unfortunately, he was wrong.

He quickly tried to comfort me, telling me that everything was okay and that nothing was going to happen to me. This was followed up with him climbing into my bed to hold me tight and trying to make me feel safe.

"Nothing is going to happen, don't worry!" he repeatedly assured me. Right!

I immediately texted my sister with the words, "SOMETHING IS IN OUR HOTEL ROOM!" When she asked me what I meant, I explained to her what had happened. I must have lain there for at least two hours, on guard and hypervigilant. I just watched and waited, hoping I would see who or what was in that room with us. My husband and I have been on a lot of vacations and have stayed in a lot of hotels and experienced nothing supernatural at any time. Finally, at about 3:00 a.m. or so, I must have drifted back to sleep.

I was awakened around 4:20 a.m. hearing my husband screaming, "Someone is trying to kill me!"

What I wanted to say to him immediately was, "Welcome to my world!"

I looked over at him and could see him physically

fighting something that wasn't there. He then jumped out of bed, and I could see the terror on his face!

He proceeded to describe exactly what happened to him, explaining that all of a sudden, he had woken to something or someone trying to crush the life out of him by placing its arms around his chest and squeezing like mad. He immediately began struggling to get free, and with one last burst of strength he did. He then told me to pack my shit because we were leaving, pronto!

I said, "Where the hell are we going to go? Everything is closed!"

Assuring him that our best bet was to wait awhile since there was nothing open at that hour, I convinced him to wait until 6:30 a.m., when the hotel started serving breakfast and stores started opening up in town. Meanwhile, I texted my sister and told her "Michael and I are being attacked in our hotel room!" At that point, a morning shower sounded extra good to me, something that might help soothe my tortured nerves. I was still pretty badly shaken up by what had happened to us and asked Michael to stay in the bathroom with me. He obliged, sitting on the toilet and checking out the morning news on the Internet. And let me just say we had every -and I mean every- light on!

At 6:30 a.m. sharp, Michael went to the lobby to get breakfast and coffee to bring back to our room. Not having slept very well, I mistakenly fell back asleep while he was gone. Suddenly, I was awakened by the sensation of something trying to squish my forehead into the pillow with the palm of its hand. When I got the nerve to open my eyes to see what was happening, I saw, for only a flash, a deep tanned-skin, damaged male face with black hair, a black beard, with yellow-stained rotten teeth. His face was about six inches from mine when he exhaled a deep breath right into my face with a horrible smell that was all but deadly. I started to scream, and he suddenly disappeared. I then started to reflect back on what I had just encountered. "OMG, I think I just saw a partially decomposed PIRATE!"

For some reason, my inner detective kicked in at that point, and I began thinking back to when I first saw the hotel online. At the time I booked our room, there were so many five-star reviews of the business's main features that I did not bother to read all the comments. After we packed up and left, I went on my computer to read those lesser reviews. There they were—several comments advising prospective guests not to stay on the third floor because it was haunted. We were in room 312!

Before we even left Hotel Haunted, however, at checkout, I felt duty-bound to give the nice young desk clerk a report on last night's happenings. I told him what happened, in great detail in order to substantiate my report and convince him that it wasn't just the feverish blabber of two people who were way too susceptible to audio-visual hallucination. I also told him, "bottom line," he should get a minister to bless the room.

He didn't believe me.

"…I saw, for only a flash, a deep tanned-skin, damaged male face with black hair, a black beard, with yellow-stained rotten teeth…"

Hubby and I then agreed that a good walk would be just what the doctor ordered to soothe our jangled nerves and forget about ghosts and pirates and things—especially 300-year-old things—that insist on sharing your bed uninvited. It soon became apparent, however, that whatever parallel universe had intersected ours the night before wasn't ready to throw in the towel just yet, for while walking through town we noticed several ghost tour excursions—the woman leading the first one we ran across helping to delay our return to three-dimensional reality by loudly claiming that Key West is really, really haunted.

She was so, so right.

12

Six Nights
of Horror

✝

Pam Mandel

2019

At the beginning of 2019, I helped to move my friend into a new home. About a twenty-minute drive from where she'd previously lived, her new household consisted of her husband, her daughter, and a friend. Although she had already lived there several weeks, she still needed to get the rest of her things moved in from storage. The plan was for me to stay with them for six nights while we completed the move. The drive was about five hours, and we arrived at her brand-new home—my eighty-pound Goldendoodle Dexter riding shotgun—at around 2:00 p.m. While my friend's husband carried my suitcase up to my second-floor bedroom, I followed behind with a few smaller items. Ever the organizer, I prepared for my week-long stay by putting everything in its proper drawer.

Pam and Dexter Hitting the Road

Once I got everything organized, I eagerly headed downstairs to catch up on the latest gossip. Halfway down the stairs, I came to an abrupt stop, courtesy of a dark, shadowy male figure coming through the wall and crossing the living room in the direction of the kitchen. He was tall, over six feet in height, with long arms, extra-long fingers, very wide shoulders, and a slender, muscular body. He walked with an extremely energetic stride and was so intensely focused on where he was going (the kitchen) that he never made direct eye contact with me. "OMG, I thought, I've barely been here twenty minutes and I've already seen a demon!"

As I arrived downstairs to join everyone, all I could think about was whether anyone else had seen it. I just couldn't believe that I was the only one to have done so. After all, it was big—big and so completely "there" that it could not possibly have joined them in the kitchen without being noticed. Then I thought about why it would even be here. It was a brand-new home with no past history. Did it have something to do with the land it's built on? Or the neighbor next door, which was the direction it came from? Considering everyone's level of excitement over the move, I just didn't want to put a damper on things, so I decided on a mum's-the-word policy. In any case, my antennae were on high alert. Thankfully, the rest of the evening was demon-free. We enjoyed a nice dinner and some great catching up time together.

There was no further demonic activity that day.

Even though I did not discuss my demon-sighting with anyone in the house, on my evening call to my husband I did decide to mention it to him. My guess at that point was that the demon was as surprised as I was that I'd seen him, and he was none too happy about it. Also, at that point my demon tally stopped at one since that was all I had seen so far.

"He walked with an extremely energetic stride and was so intensely focused on where he was going…"

NIGHT 1

It had been a long day with hours spent behind the wheel and tons of other activities, and bedtime beckoned! Dexter and I got into bed and got ready to watch some TV. (Note: Yes, Dexter loves watching television). The minute that TV is turned on, he stretches out right in front of it intently watching for that one animal to show himself. You might remember the events described in one of my previous stories (Chapter 4). Because of those experiences, I always sleep with a night light on in my bedroom. At around 1:00 a.m., having fallen into a deep sleep after all the driving we'd done that day, I was abruptly awakened by a very creepy feeling. I was suddenly afraid, so afraid that I opened one watchful eye and kept the other one closed in an attempt to feign sleep. With that one open eye I glanced around the room, focusing on my dog to see if he'd reacted to whatever it was that had woken me up. He continued with his doggie snoring in his inimitably cute doggie style, apparently unaffected by whatever it was that had penetrated my deep sleep.

And then it started.

The bed shook.

Now we were both awake with our eyes wide open. Suddenly, a very large black mass was moving from the doorway towards me, silhouetted against the new home's freshly painted white walls. While the words PRAY! PRAY! PRAY bombarded my brain, I flipped my body over and hid my face in the pillow, continuing to call on the Lord of All for help. Eventually, the creepy feeling subsided, and after a couple hours I was able to fall asleep.

"…a very large black mass was moving from the doorway towards me, silhouetted against the new home's freshly painted white walls…"

The next day, despite what I'd been through the previous night, I decided not to say a word to anyone about it. I just didn't want to say anything that might puncture the bubble of excitement that had engulfed everyone. As I was coming down the staircase, I heard someone whisper to me. I stopped to listen but didn't hear anything further. I could not understand what the four words were but only that it was a deep voice and each word had one syllable. I thought "OMG, what is it with this staircase?" As far as the other people in the house were concerned, I continued to keep radio silence regarding the strange things that were happening to me!

NIGHT 2

Nighttime was approaching, and I have to tell you that it was definitely not something I was looking forward to. Being alone upstairs in my bedroom was beginning to be a very uncomfortable experience for me, to say the least. I attended to my new routine: get doggie, lock the bedroom door, turn on the nightstand light, and turn up the volume on the TV set so loud that I couldn't hear anything coming from outside the bedroom. Well, 1:20 a.m. rolled around, and I was lying there wide awake with the TV still blaring. All I could focus on was an extremely loud noise—so loud that I could hear this over my TV— coming from outside my bedroom. Its point of origin seemed to be the loft down the hall.

"OMG, I thought, what the hell is that?" I muted the TV and just lay there listening. It sounded like a whole crew of professional movers were hard at work in the loft. Thinking that the racket they/it/whatever were making would be even worse downstairs, I wondered if anyone else heard it. My curiosity got the best of me and I concluded, "get yourself out of bed and see what is going on." Maybe by some small chance this wasn't yet another episode of *The Twilight Zone* taking over my life! In any case, it was time to find out. So, I cautiously opened the door. The noise stopped! I closed the door. The noise started. I opened the door and entered the hallway and just stood there. Again, it was completely silent. To this day I cannot come up with the right words to describe the feeling that had overtaken me. "Creepy" just seems to fall short of doing justice to the energy that was in the air.

Fear grabbed ahold of me from my head to my toes as I walked to the edge of the loft to have a good look at what was going on downstairs. Leaning over to try to get a good look, I heard the loudest female voice coming from behind me scream, "Get away from the edge!"

I quickly stepped away from the edge and turned around to see who it was and there, about ten feet away, stood the most unbelievable creature I had ever seen— and believe me, I've had my share of them. It was darker than dark, just like the abovementioned one. This one, however, had two horns on its head. My first impulse was to give myself a good smack to see if I was awake. Instead, I just stood there staring at him while reminding myself to breathe, breathe, and then I told myself to run, run back to my room and lock that bedroom door as fast as I could.

We do what we can in moments of peril, and maybe we shouldn't be too hard on ourselves when we look back on the silly things we do to save our skins when our very lives seem threatened. I don't know why I thought locking my door would keep Freddie Kruger 2 out, but what was even funnier (or seems so now that I was out of danger) was my dog Dexter running right behind me and almost knocking me over as I ran back to my room. Dexter and I got into bed, and I lay there wondering what the hell was going on in this house. And then the thought gripped me. Just who was it who screamed, "Get away from the edge"? Who was warning me? The voice I heard was a female, could it have been my mom? Was the black shadow with horns going to throw me over the edge?

"…there, about ten feet away, stood the most unbelievable creature I had ever seen…"

After night two of the Late-Night Horror Show, I decided to bring my girlfriend up to speed on what was going on. I started off slowly by saying that she had a wee bit of a problem in the house. Alas, that tack just didn't seem to be working, so after a few minutes the soft shoe approach gave way to "You have an infestation of demons in this house!" For some reason she didn't act surprised because, even though she hadn't seen anything, on several occasions she had heard whispering—as had her daughter—when no one else was present. Unfortunately, though, she could never make out what the voices were saying either.

Let me just say that, by now, when going up or down the stairs I had both hands on that handrail. The fact that my ghoulish neighbors were too close for comfort was more than just a little disconcerting, and at my age I didn't want to take a nosedive down twenty steps with no landing to break the fall.

NIGHT 3

My favorite time of the night was coming around, that time when all the WTH moments that happened to me over a period of sixty years were happening night after night. I followed a strict routine when retiring for the night along with Dexter: locking the bedroom door, turning the nightstand light on, and turning up the TV's volume so loud that I couldn't hear anything else. Those bright white walls had become annoying by now, acting as a backdrop that made those darker-than-dark demons even scarier! When

SIX NIGHTS OF HORROR

3:00 a.m. rolled around, the bed started to shake again, so I thought Dexter might be moving around while indulging himself in a self-grooming session. I raised my head to get a good look at him and. lo and behold, there stood a huge—and I mean huge—demon right next to me. And to make things worse, the two-foot long black grasshoppers he'd brought with him were crawling up the wall and across the ceiling. By now, after three consecutive nights of this, I was utterly freaked out. I sat up in bed, and in a firm voice said, "In the name of Jesus, get out!" He didn't move! OMG, now what? Although I was deathly afraid and close to hysteria, I didn't want to show it, so I closed my eyes and started to pray like I'd never prayed before.

When I opened my eyes, everything was gone.

NIGHT 4

Again, it's my favorite time of the evening: Late-Night Horror Show time. Dexter and I have the drill down pat by now: up the stairs into the bedroom, lock the door, nightstand light on, and TV volume turned up so loud that I was just about deaf to any sound(s) coming from outside the room.

But first I had to go to the bathroom.

While sitting on the toilet I turned to my left, and guess who was coming through the bathroom door? Yes, the demon with the horns! He just stood there and watched me as I went into full-fledged panic mode. I thought WTH! At this point I knew he was fully trying the intimidate me coming into

THE HAUNTINGS OF TWO SISTERS

such a small private space such as a bathroom. I just sat there knowing that I would have to go through him to get the hell out! Before I had to make that walk, he disappeared.

I lay there in bed, trying to think of a way to tell my friend that something had come up unexpectedly. I needed to cut my trip short. So far, it's been three nights of horror, and it's really beginning to drain me emotionally and rob me of the deep sleep I so badly needed after moving her items from her storage space to the house.

As I watched TV, I noticed a huge dog by my bed, a dog even bigger than eighty-pound Dexter. His coat was midnight-black, and he was sniffing away at the plateful of snacks on my nightstand. I thought, "This just keeps getting better and better. What's next?"

Blessed with a newfound spirit of resolve, I resolved that what was going to come next was my packing my bags in the morning and getting the hell out of there.

I sat my girlfriend down the next morning in order to break the news to her about my having to cut my stay short because of an emergency. She was in a chatty mood, so I just let her talk away without interruption about her daughter and her friend (whom my husband and I had known for over twenty years). As she went on about nearly everything in her life and then some, I started to zone out. I began to reflect instead on what I had seen these past four nights. I realized that it had been almost sixteen years since we went through something just like this (see Chapter 4)—the demon characters, the darker-than-dark shadow man, the big black grasshoppers with four legs, and the huge hell hound.

What was going on here?

It was a new home, so could the culprit be the land rather than the house that was built on it? But then a light bulb switched on in my brain as I thought of something whose importance had escaped me all those years ago. I remembered that the friend had stayed at our home just a couple weeks before all the creepiness started. I'd been thoroughly confused at the time because we had lived there over two years with nothing happening and then, out of the blue, a posse of demons ended up ruining our home and causing us to move. That single memory convinced me that an entirely new tack was needed!

So, I changed course.

I was going to stay, after all, and continue to help my girlfriend. Since nights five and six were guaranteed to be off the horror charts, however, I decided to fortify myself with some heavy-duty sleeping pills. I was ready to go to full la-la-land in order to shield myself from this nightmare. In order to do so I needed to be at least half "out of it."

NIGHT 5

It was that time of night, and by now Dexter and I had the nightly routine down cold. As far as the evening's television fare, I had to nix the very idea of watching any crime, horror, or thriller-type movies. By that point, they were just way too close to the reality of my life. What I really needed instead was a dose of some really good comedy, the kind that makes you laugh so hard that you forget why you ever stopped laughing in the first place. So, all ready for la-la-land with the help of two extra strength sleeping pills, I made myself comfortable and got ready to watch our funny movie with my furry buddy and faithful companion stretched out beside me. By the time the movie was over, I was a little deeper in la-la-land than was comfortable, but what the heck, there were no horror sightings to report—so mission accomplished!

I was groggy when I woke up the next morning, so I decided to take only one extra-strength sleeping pill that night since I had a five-hour drive ahead of me the next morning. On my way downstairs to join everyone, I heard a very loud growl in the vicinity of the window that overlooked the staircase. I knew it couldn't be Dexter since he was out playing with my girlfriend's dog, and furthermore I had never heard Dexter make a sound that even remotely resembled that one. I continued down the stairs, gripping the railing with both hands in case someone had the bright idea of giving me a little unrequested help making the trip more quickly than I wanted to.

NIGHT 6

Finally.

Here we go again for the last time, the last night of our Late-Night Horror Show! After feasting hungrily on another much-needed comedy and easing my way into dreamland, this time with only one extra-strength sleeping pill, I was packed and ready to head out by 6:00 the next morning. I was able to get to sleep with only one pill, but not deeply enough to be oblivious of what was going on around me. I could still feel the presence of that dreadful demon pack in my sleep but, with the help of mother's little helper, did not wake up to see them this time. Although I might have attained the desired state of total oblivion with two pills, I knew that if I doubled the dosage I would severely lower the chances of having a safe drive home.

While saying goodbye to my girlfriend, I mentioned that if I ever came to visit again, I'd book a hotel room. What had gone on during my week in her house just wasn't something I looked forward to experiencing again—no offense intended.

NEVER AGAIN!

Note: In Chapter 15 "I am Never Alone," I mention a few demonic attacks that took place a few weeks after I returned home from this trip. Did they follow me home?

Chapter 4 and Chapter 12 (which cover incidents separated by 16 years), have two things in common—"Same demons" and "The Friend."

13

Enjoy the
Ride, Ken!

✝

Karen Pena

2001 - 2019

After those horrific hauntings I went through including the parade of elephants on the staircase (see Chapter 3), I needed a fresh start, preferably in a house without the memories that continued to haunt me. That is when, 1999, we decided to move from San Jose to a brand-new home located in Brentwood, California.

Since Mom had only a small portion of her heart working and Dad needed help with her, we purchased a house that was large enough for my husband, me, our two teenagers, and my parents. That way I could be there for both of them as needed.

One night, not long after we'd moved, I woke up to an apparition of a former co-worker. In his early fifties, he wore light gray pants, a pink dress shirt and a dark gray belt. While standing in my bathroom doorway, he kept saying, "I'm sorry, I'm sorry," while staring at me intently. He then walked from the bathroom doorway to my side of the bed and began to talk to me. Not hearing a word, all I could focus on, however, was the unexplained reason for his visit. What the hell was he doing in our bedroom? These thoughts crowded my mind until I realized that if I was really seeing him, and this wasn't a dream, then something bad must have happened to him. By that time, I was ready and eager to listen to what he had to say, but unfortunately, he vanished.

For days I couldn't get my mind off what had just happened, my thoughts switching back and forth between "Could he be dead at only fifty-two years old" and "If he was dead, why was he here in our home?" After two weeks of mental ping pong, my curiosity got the better of me, and I called my brother-in-law—who had worked with him—to get some information about my nocturnal visitor. Shocked to hear that he had passed away a couple weeks before, I inquired about the cause of death.

Unknown.

Not long after that, I started to have the feeling that I was not alone. My life was so busy then, however, with six of us under the same roof, that I just didn't give it much thought.

In December 2002, we decided to move yet again with our parents from Brentwood, California to Las Vegas. The setup could hardly have been better. They had their own apartment above our garage but were still close enough in case they needed help. I was glad to see them enjoying their morning casino visits during which they loved Vegas's ubiquitous penny slot machines and generous breakfast buffets. Life was good for them!

On March 4, 2008, Mom's world was turned upside down when our Dad passed away from a heart attack. My sister thought it best to spend most nights with Mom during this difficult period—especially on April 7, 2008, which would have been Dad's eightieth birthday. Early that morning, my mom and my sister were awakened by a barrage of hard knocks (seven to be exact) on the headboard of the bed they were sharing. Pam wondered what was going on, but Mom knew instinctively that it was Dad letting her know he was there with her.

On another occasion, I went out to the patio to water the flowers one evening, and there was Dad just staring at me, looking just like he did before he died. My mom had left the day before to go and visit my sister in California, the first time she had done so since Dad's passing.

He looked at me angrily and said, "Where is your Mother?" and I explained that she was with Pam.

The next time I saw him was about two months later, again on the patio. This time, however, he looked to be about twenty-five years old. His age was easy to guess because he looked just like he did in my parents' wedding pictures. These visitations were repeated several times, and they were always about our mom. It was plain to see from all this that his concern for her was never-ending. By this time, I needed no further convincing, knowing full well that the many shadows in the house could not have belonged to anyone other than Dad.

Our Parents Celebrating their Wedding Day on November 17, 1951

One week, Pam came down to see Mom and me. Happy to share Mom's bedroom, the two of them reminded me of nothing more than two teenage girls at a perpetual slumber party. On many occasions, when I walked past their room with the door open, I'd get a glimpse of them snuggling while watching TV. One of those times, as they were lying in bed, my sister spotted a tall man peeking around the corner of the bedroom door. When she shared that bit of news with me the next morning, I wasted no time in letting her know who the mystery guest was.

"It's Dad, Pam. I think he's moved back in with us!"

To which she replied, "It certainly didn't look like him."

My sister then informed me that in addition to the man who peeked around the corner, there were several other spirits in my house, including my husband's grandparents as well as that of a family friend. Although she had never seen any of the three spirits before, she was still able to describe them to me perfectly. The man who peeked around the corner, though, remained unidentified.

Another memorable ghostly encounter took place about a year later when Mom and I visited my sister. We were all out on her back patio, enjoying the weather, when my sister spotted a man walking across the kitchen. The patio door was left open for the dogs to go in and out. He walked up to the glass door, stuck his head out, and looked straight at me with an intensity that threw my sister off balance! She told me that she knew he was there just for me since he just stood there shaking his head while staring (or maybe glaring, to be more accurate) right at me.

My guess was that he didn't like the fact that I was smoking.

After my sister treated my mother and me to a loudly exclaimed "Wow, who was that?" I asked my sister who she was referring to. She filled me in on what she had seen, letting me know that this looked exactly like the guy who had peeked around the corner during her last visit. When I asked for a description, she immediately focused on his full head of hair. Light brown with light blonde streaks, parted on the side and flowing down past his ears. She insisted that it was the most beautiful hair she'd ever seen on a guy. It was only when she followed up with a blow-by-blow description, though, that I knew exactly who it was.

Then she dropped the bombshell. No, it wasn't Dad who'd decided to drop in at my house. Someone else had taken up residence with me, and that someone else was none other than Ken.

That explained a lot. The many dots were now starting to connect themselves for me at warp speed. At last, things were starting to make sense now. The shadow figures in our Brentwood house that continued after moving to Las Vegas, the unforgettable sound of something coming up the stairs—had he been with me since I'd first saw him standing in that bathroom door?

My grandkids, aged six and seven, moved in with us through a fifty-percent custody arrangement right after our son's divorce in 2013. From a second-floor bedroom loft, my grandson would often hear the sound of someone running upstairs at around 2:00 a.m. It began to wear him down to the point that he started developing a case of nerves. On one occasion, someone even grabbed my granddaughter's feet while she was lying in bed, and on another occasion, she actually woke up to a little girl singing happily to the bunny in the bunny cage I'd set up in her bedroom—a performance that had several encores.

When I told my sister about the little girl, she informed me that she had seen Ken walking through her house hand-in-hand with the child.

Before then, my grandkids had had a live-in babysitter who loved them very much and was a big part of their lives. They were only four and five when he passed away at age thirty-two. He had been very protective of them while still a dweller on this plane, something that apparently continued after he passed on. One time, after their dad had punished them for talking after bedtime, he went to take a shower, and the shower curtain and rod fell on top of him without any help from him. Their dad was totally convinced that it was not an accident but something that was, intentional and deliberate.

Once, when I woke up in the middle of the night and, as I made my way downstairs to get a glass of water, I could hear people talking away as soon as I reached the landing. After I'd stopped for at least a minute to listen, I could hear one of the male voices dominating the conversation. To confirm my first thought, that someone had left the TV on when they went to bed, I continued down the stairs and made my way to the living room only to find that the TV was off—no sound at all. To add shock to surprise, the minute I turned the corner and walked into the family room, the silence was so complete that it was downright creepy.

There was a very negative energy in the house, one that I could feel deeply at the end of the day when my daytime survival mechanisms weren't at their strongest. Often, I'd be sitting on my bed, getting ready to get comfy under the covers, when I'd feel an evil presence. Typically, it would come and go in cycles. One night, while heading down the stairs for a late-night snack, I could feel that energy following so closely that my blood began to chill. In order to avoid losing my balance and taking a tumble down the stairs, I gripped the railing fiercely with both hands and made my way down to the ground floor of the house. Just as I got to the kitchen, I could feel it coming up real close behind again when all of a sudden, I heard this enormous, explosive popping sound.

"OMG," I thought. "What was that?"

Here's another strange happening. We have a part pit bull named Cash. Like many of that breed and/or mix, he has never been afraid of anything or anyone. At a certain point, however, my husband and I started to notice a change in his behavior. For example, he would be playing with his ball, running all over the place, and then all of a sudden, he'd drop it, jump up on the bed, and cuddle right up against me. It was obvious that something just wasn't right in his world. This state of affairs got progressively worse until, on more than one occasion, he'd start trembling for no apparent reason. You know what they say about spirits in your house: your animals with their sixth sense are the proverbial canaries in the coal mine when it comes to sensing their presence.

At other times I'd be all alone in my bedroom, with

no one else in the house, and hear a whole lot of noise coming from the downstairs room where my husband had set up a ladder for some sort of do-it-yourself renovation. When I went down to check out the noise, lo and behold, the ladder had mysteriously migrated to the other side of the room! All I could think of at that point was KEN!

It has been approximately twenty years now since Ken has passed and believe it or not, he is still a frequent visitor at our home—sometimes entering my field of vision as he walks through the house checking on everything. When I visit my sister, she sees him joining in at times and even taking car rides in our backseat with us. I guess someday I will know why, but until then, enjoy the ride, Ken!

14

From a
Husband's View
✝

Michael Mandel

One thing I want to make perfectly clear: I deeply believe in God, Jesus Christ, Heaven, Hell, angels, demons, etc. Ghosts roam this earth. They are not only haunting old Victorian mansions but also modern penthouses, luxury yachts, bars, and restaurants, and are in every corner of this world. Some people can see them;

most cannot. Unfortunately, these gifted people can also see demons, and the people who have the misfortune of being able to see and feel these monsters truly have my condolences. I believe these despicable entities are regurgitated straight from hell and are here on Earth to cause us nothing but pain. They are here to recruit troops.

That said, when I met my wife Pam in 1996, little did I know that I would be in for the ride of my life. She is a person who loves to laugh, and that's what attracted me to her. She was smart, energetic, and had a real zest to experience everything she could from life. I had no knowledge of her "ghostly" past, no knowledge of her premonitions, no knowledge of her run-ins with shadow people or angelic beings. But she did warn me when we started getting serious that she had this connection with the other side, that she could "see" things. Looking back on those early years, I think she wanted to ease me into her spiritual world gracefully. I didn't listen. Instead I was caught up in her sense of humor and just how green those eyes were. My attitude was "Yeah, right, whatever you say." But as it turned out, I should have heeded the warning because it was dead on. She really had no choice in the matter, but I was thrown into this vortex nearly right from the get-go.

My background and sightings in the spiritual world have been basically non-existent. Before Pam, I can honestly say that I had never experienced anything supernatural. But like one's belief in God, I still believe in the afterlife as well as all things supernatural without actually experiencing anything myself in this domain. I had never even known anyone who had this "gift" before, but I had always been intrigued with the spiritual world growing up. I can remember staying up late on a Saturday night in the '60s watching *Creature Features* and getting the crap scared out of me. Later on, movies like *The Exorcist* and *Poltergeist* took fear to the next level. Like most kids growing up, we even had an old 19th-century house deep in the woods that everyone believed to be haunted. When it burned to the ground, my friends and I were on the front line to watch the fire department try and save it, to no avail.

I lived for Halloween, and as you can guess, it was my favorite holiday. It wasn't so much the candy but running around in the dark with a bunch of other ghouls, trying to be scary and just acting stupid. Who knew that fifty years later I would be living a real Halloween every day of my life in Pam's World? The things that she has seen and experienced in her life are staggering. Most of the time, it's just another day of ghosts and goblins for her, but there have been times when things have become quite frightening and even dangerous.

You have to understand that ninety-five percent of the time she experiences anything supernatural, I don't see or hear anything. It doesn't mean it's not there; I simply was not born with the gift. For instance, we'll be watching TV and out of the blue: "Did you see that? A dark shadow just went across the doorway."

Mr. Oblivious, of course, saw nothing. A lot of husbands would say their wives are crazy, but I know better. It's not just because of pure faith. Her experiences have been going on for sixty years, and to be honest with you, nobody has the patience to make up stories for sixty years. Besides, I know my wife and she is as honest as the day is long and expects those around her to be the same.

There have been perhaps three or four incidents over the years that have involved me. A few have been very minor, but nonetheless unexplainable. For instance, we heard our names called out at the same time, in different parts of the house, when neither one of us spoke. Creepy. Then there was the time when we both heard a dog drinking out of the water bowl, but all of our dogs are on the bed with us. Sitting in the living room one night, watching television, I heard something over by the sink in the kitchen. It sounded like a portion of a dog's metal collar hitting the side of the sink. I glanced over and saw a flash of a dog's large head drop down, dark in color, and then it was gone. For a moment I was confused because our dogs are sable in color and were nowhere around. What was it? Pam has experienced many episodes of a "demon" dog walking through the house growling at her. Was my visual that same dog? I have no other explanation.

Speaking of dogs, we have had three or four canine family members we've had to put down over the years. It's always horrible, something that is going to happen if you allow dogs into your life, but there have been instances when those deceased canines have made an appearance again back in our lives. There has been more than one occasion when I have been sitting on the couch, standing by the kitchen sink, or just rummaging around in the fridge, when I have felt something rub up against my lower leg, looking down, always seeing nothing. Again, my dogs are nowhere to be seen. I personally have never seen a visual of any of these occurrences, but not Pam. Many times, she has seen one of our deceased fur children happily walking across the floor looking for God knows what. Both of us agree that it makes us happy to know that they are still around to make themselves known to us, but at the same time, a little unsettling.

I would like to talk about the main event, at least where I am concerned. Pam discussed this in the chapter about our trip to Key West, but I would like to interject my interpretation about this eerie and very bizarre encounter. We had no idea that night that we were about to stay in a genuinely haunted hotel; believe me, that was not our intention. We just wanted a place near the action that was clean, modern, and user-friendly.

So, when we hunkered down for the night after a long day of island activities, we were tired and in no mood for any ghostly hanky-panky. After Pam was, let's just say, sensually attacked, I thought, okay, I will come to your rescue and protect you from whatever was invading your space. Remember, similar things have happened to us before, and I have always enjoyed being the knight in shining armor helping the damsel in distress. Boy, was I wrong this time! After cuddling up to her and telling her all the appropriate things to ease her mind, I drifted off to sleep rather quickly. I was awakened abruptly! Unable to comprehend what was happening to me, I felt two muscular arms tightening around my chest in a desperate attempt to stop me from breathing. I fought back wildly, flailing my arms about and trying to break away from this unseen attacker. I heard nothing, saw nothing, and even smelled nothing, but the attack on me was quite real and like nothing I had ever experienced before.

I was finally able to break free and bolted like a cannonball out of bed. I stood up, looked around, unable to comprehend what had just taken place. I know I was not dreaming, and I sure as hell had not lost my mind . . . at least not yet. That's when I finally yelled at Pam, "Get your shit, we're getting out of here now!" Fighting an attacker is one thing, but an unseen one, come on, really.

I guess I'm not as tough as I thought I was. Through the years when Pam was experiencing these phenomena, I always thought if they came after me, I'd let them have it. Yeah, right. You really don't know what it's like until it happens to you personally. She's a pretty tough lady. And one thing's for sure, I got a lot more than I bargained for when I married her.

Pam and Michael on their Wedding Day on February 14, 1998

I Am
Never Alone

✝

Pam Mandel

You might wonder what everyday life is like for someone who can see and occasionally hear dead people. Believe me when I tell you it is the last thing on my mind during the course of my busy day. So, bear with me as I take a few moments to give you a short rundown in the hopes of convincing you that I am somewhat "normal."

Living a very demanding life, working full time in the financial department of non-profits, and being a woman of faith helps me to be all the more thankful for the many things life has to offer.

One of the most homebound enjoyments I have is decorating our home. Loving different colors and textures, I sometimes venture well outside the box of my comfort zone! There are times when my freewheeling approach works great, and other times when I can't help but wonder what I was thinking! This is usually when my sister comes to my rescue with a lot of encouragement, plus the necessary changes needed to pull me way back into that comfort zone. We not only make a great decorating team but also work well together as a ghostbuster team!

Koi pond with Michael, Pam and Watson

My hubby and I spend many hours beautifying our gardens, and even though it is a labor of love for both of us, Michael puts so much more time into our yards than I do. When we first got married, we built a very large koi pond and loaded it with lots of koi and red-eared-slider turtles. Even though koi enthusiasts say it is a no-no to mix the two species, in this case they got along quite well. Back then, my main ambition was to be on the annual pond tour and we actually made it during 2002, with our pond featured in our local newspaper. I was beside myself with excitement, so much so that I decided to write an article later that year for the *Koi USA* magazine. It had to do with our big Old English Sheepdog's habit of sticking his nose in the water. All the Koi would congregate around it and actually start sucking on it, thinking it was dinnertime, so I called it "A Nose in a Pond." My article was published in *Koi USA* magazine (November/ December 2002 issue).

One of my other hobbies is fishing. I just love it! Being the boy my father always wanted but never had, he started me on the road to becoming a dedicated angler at age four. Although both my sister and I were taken along on these fishing trips, Karen just wasn't into it like I was. Her solution was to bring a good book along and very quietly sit there reading while Dad and I worked hard trying to reel in the next great catch. I was so into it, in fact, that I insisted that Dad change my bait every five minutes if I was not getting any bites. But guess who always caught the fish? You got it—my sister! It still cracks me up today when I think about it. But now that the pond tour is off my bucket list, my number one goal on the top of that list is to catch that ever-elusive marlin! I am batting 0-for-3 on that one, catching many other big fish but no marlin on those three expeditions so far. I guess this is sort of my own personal Moby Dick, and I'm still eagerly waiting for that big catch!

Before my husband married me, he had never owned an animal. I laugh because, being the avid animal lover that I am, we have had up to four dogs at one time along with rabbits, birds, fish, and turtles. My husband (now that he has had dogs) and I can't even conceive of ever being animal-less, especially when it comes to dogs. Eight years ago, we added to our family an eight-week-old Goldendoodle that was the highest energy dog we had ever had. We called him Dexter, and what a terror he was and if you can believe it, still is. His energy level is so high that we seriously wondered if his hurricane-force energy would do us in eventually. My husband even remarked at one point that getting him was the biggest mistake of our lives! Not wanting to go through that again at this stage of our lives, we now (in our *wiser years* hopefully) plan to rescue older dogs that need a home. That way it's a win-win for everybody.

I can't leave out "Shark Week"! Karen and I are devout Shark Week fans! She started watching it back in 1989, just after its first year on the air. Not long after that, I was right there with her. Having waited in line back in 1975 at our local drive-in movie theater for over four hours to see the opening night of *Jaws,* we were hooked almost right from the start! I even have my shark costumes I wear while I watch it.

The one thing I have missed more than anything during the Coronavirus pandemic is people! I love to be around people and share good times with them—so much so, admittedly, I can be a live wire at times. Once, in fact, I laughed so hard when visiting and fishing with my sister that I actually passed out. I still kind of wonder if she thought that I'd had a heart attack—at least until she finally realized that it was yet another episode of me laughing uncontrollably. So you see, my paranormal travels aside, I am really very close to being normal!

For years I have grappled with the fact that if I open up to others about my gift of seeing things on the other side, they would immediately start to think of me as a little crazy—okay, more than a little—so for the most part I keep my mouth shut. Before I reached the age of sixty, there were very few people with whom I felt comfortable and trusted enough to share it with. It hasn't been until now, in my mid-sixties, that I feel secure enough to freely talk about it.

Now to go a little bit further back in time, I was twenty-four when I married my first husband, and my son was born a year later in 1982. With my husband being a minister, the last thing I ever wanted to discuss with him was my ability to see dead people. Not wanting even to imagine his reaction, it was something I never talked about. As a result, I totally closed myself off from other dimensions during the fourteen years we were married. Yes, there were times I did see and experience the paranormal, but I chose to be silent.

When I met my second and current husband at age forty in 1996, I decided I wanted things to be different regarding my extrasensory side. Simply put, I was no longer willing to hide what I saw and heard from my companion. When we started to get serious about our relationship and I decided to share my gift with him, he just smiled and said nothing. Since he immediately changed the subject, I concluded by the end of our evening together that our relationship had been concluded, too. When I got home on that windy and gray March night, I just lay in bed for what seemed like ages, counting the ways in which I'd really messed up. I was so sure he thought I was absolutely crazy that I even thought of calling him that night and asking him if he liked my early April Fool's joke! The thing was that I wanted my next forty years to be about who I really was and not who I wasn't. So, I figured at that point, all I could reasonably do was wait and see if he called again.

Okay, spoiler alert. You already know he's my second husband, so there goes the surprise. He called! We were married on February 14, 1998, and our first round of shared paranormal experiences started that same year (see Chapter 3). I think that was when he really started to believe me because he'd learned that there were just too many things going on that could not be explained. When you live with someone who can see and hear extraordinary things, sometimes you yourself start to have experiences as well—and that is exactly what happened. Little by little, paranormal experiences started happening for the first time since he married me. These occurrences succeeded in breaking the ice for him. Although not nearly as extensive as mine, they are still nothing to scoff at. In fact, this is hardly the case. They run the gamut from hearing voices to full-fledged demonic attacks—with many other occurrences in between. When I sit back and reflect on how my husband's life has changed since marrying me, I chuckle because I can't determine whether it is for the better or the worse. With all the animals, my bucket list items, and ghosts included, I think that is up for debate!

As I've stated, my daily life is pretty busy with my working full time, so spirits really need to put some effort into getting my attention. A few of their attention-getting techniques are throwing something across the room, pulling my hair, grabbing my leg, turning lights on and off, or staring from a reasonable distance until I have a weird feeling of being watched. There are times when I can hear them talking. At times, they are all talking at once and so fast that I can't pick up a thing. Sometimes in their group discussion, there will be one voice that is more boisterous than the others. The timing varies as there may be several occurrences within the space of a single week or several months may go by without one happening. The fact of the matter is you never really know when the next paranormal experience is going to occur. If there is any predictability, it is the unpredictability of it all. Although some of these incidents happen during the day, far too many occur at night when they can really, truly freak me out. Given a choice, I'd take daytime paranormal experiences any day of the week over those that happen on dark, eerie nights!

My main challenge is to be open enough to sense and welcome the good spirits but, at the same time, protect myself from the bad ones. As you can see from our stories, this can really be an issue until you learn how to protect yourself from the evil spirits that are out there. When I look back even to a year ago, the terror and panic I would feel was so overwhelming. I soon realized the more fear I showed the more they came at me. I was only fueling their energy. It isn't something you just learn, but it is a daily process that requires constant dependence on God's protection. At times I snuggle up tight against my husband when I feel a bad spirit. He knows the drill and is always glad to help out with a steadying hand placed on mine, or at other times he would ask me if I was okay.

You would think that after all these years I would be more comfortable seeing ghosts, but I'm not. Although in principle, I don't usually panic when I see them, that immediately changes if I start to feel danger. When it comes to these unexpected encounters, I don't think I will ever be comfortable with them. On the other hand, maybe you're not supposed to be!

In the end, though, I am very grateful to God for my gift. Largely because I know our loved ones are still around continuing to check in on birthdays, weddings, and other family ceremonies.

Following are some recent experiences—daily events for the most part—that are not covered elsewhere in our book.

LADY IN RED

While working at my desk, all of a sudden, I felt some-one's presence. Looking up to check out my surroundings, I saw a woman that I have never seen before just standing there staring straight at me. She had red hair, a red leisure suit, and even had on big round red glasses. Usually, once I notice them, they immediately disappear, but this Lady in Red hung around and started to talk. She was talking so fast I could not understand anything she said. It would certainly have been nice if she repeated it slower.

She did not.

SHADOW MAN CHILL

When Mom was living with us, hearing a noise, I got up to check on her. As I came out of my bedroom going towards hers, unknowingly I walked right through a spirit. As I went through it, I immediately turned around and there he was, just standing there looking at me. It had the shape of a very large male with a long torso. I felt a glacial chill run through me, a chill that lingered even after he faded away right before my eyes.

DECOMPOSED LADY IN WHITE

While I was asleep facing the edge of the bed, I felt someone or something touch me. Opening my eyes to see who it was, there was a short lady wearing a white gown with long black wet-looking hair. Part of her face was decomposed, and as she leaned over me, I noticed that her fingers and nails were extremely long. When I bolted upright, she moved backwards, at which point I let out a scream that was so loud it actually freaked me out. It woke the entire household. I had already seen her a couple months earlier on her way from the hallway into the living room. At that time, however, I only got a side view. But let me assure you that it was nowhere near as terrifying as seeing her face to face from a distance of only a few inches. A few nights later when I was away for the evening, my husband actually heard something let out the most God-awful scream, waking him out of a sound sleep. He searched the entire house and did not find anything. Could it have been her?

"...a short lady wearing a white gown with long black wet-looking hair..."

VOICE ON A RANCH

My husband and I were taking care of the animals on a friend's ranch while she went away for a long weekend. Michael was very excited about it because she had a horse and he could not wait to feed him the carrots she had left in the refrigerator for just that. Along with the horse, she had a cat, a pond full of koi, and about forty chickens. Just after I collected all the eggs from the chicken coop and brought them into the kitchen to clean and put away, all of a sudden, a loud man's voice said a complete sentence.

I could not understand what he said, so I replied, "What do you need, Michael?"

No answer. So, I headed towards the back door to find out what he needed. That is when I saw him across the property, yes, feeding the horse those carrots. I was shocked there was no one else in the house but me, or at least that is what I thought, so I checked everywhere— found no one. My friend's husband had passed away a few months before—could it have been him?

THE FLYING HALF-INDIAN

One night I awoke at around 12:30 a.m. with a very uncomfortable feeling, so I just lay there waiting for whatever was going to happen next. There was a Native American man with just half a body extending from his head to his stomach, flying from my dressing room into my bedroom and out the bedroom door after making a very tight turn and actually ducking to get through the doorway. He had salt-and-pepper hair down to his shoulders and wore a big, black, floppy hat. His nose was huge, and he had extremely high cheekbones. I just watched him, wondering what and who he was. Half a body and flying! A couple weeks later I was telling my neighbor about it, and she saved me the trouble of describing him by doing it for me before I could get more than a few words out. I was shocked (again) to say the least.

"He had salt-and-pepper hair down to his shoulders and wore a big, black, floppy hat..."

My mom was living with us at the time, and one day shortly after my encounter, I came home from work to find her sitting on the couch, frozen with fear. I asked her what was wrong, and she told me that she had seen someone in the house earlier. After looking under every nook and cranny, though, she still couldn't find him. When I asked her to describe him, guess what? Yes, it was the same Native American man I'd seen three weeks earlier. I assured her that there was no reason to worry or be afraid since it was only a ghost.

She retorted, "Is that supposed to make me feel better?"

We both got a big laugh over that!

THREE AMIGOS

And then there were the Three Amigos—I was awakened by the familiar feeling of being watched. Since I didn't see anything at first, I rolled over and looked in the opposite direction, and voilá, there they were—all three of them. There were two girls and one boy, all in their mid-teens, and all three were staring right at me. They wore period pieces, outfits of a matching pale yellow. The boy had on a wide waistband and white shirt, and his trousers were held up by suspenders. The girls had pale yellow skirts and white blouses. All three had light brown hair, and the girls' hair was twisted into long braids. I was calmer this time since we had a considerable distance between us. So, I just held their gaze for sixty seconds—a period of time which may not seem all that long unless you're staring at a ghost who has decided to join you in your bedroom in the middle of the night. Then they started to talk. One of them shared with me that they had been reincarnated several times. They disappeared shortly after that, and I never saw them again.

"There were two girls and one boy, all in their mid-teens, and all three were staring right at me..."

GRIEF OUTRAGE

A few weeks after my mom passed, the realization that she was gone started to really sink in. One night while hubby was away, I woke up and started to cry. Being alone, I let it all out, and the tears just would not stop coming. Afterwards I just lay there on my back, totally exhausted, when suddenly I noticed a red light in the form of a foot-and-a-half-long straight line with two red eyes on it. It flew in from the bedroom doorway to the bottom of my bed and then stopped and just hovered about seven feet off the ground. My fearful reaction to this appearance of unadulterated evil quickly gave way to a feeling of outrage. The fact that this whatever-it-was could barge into my bedroom and attempt to take advantage of my grief was outrageous. It was time to fight back, so I immediately shouted, "Get out!" and started to pray. It disappeared and never returned.

BACKYARD INTRUDER

I was lying in bed watching television. My husband was just getting out of the shower when, out of the blue, I notice on our security camera right next to the TV a man running across the backyard. I couldn't help but wonder how he managed to get over the fence or through the locked gate that led to our yard. He looked like he was in his late thirties, wearing peach-colored shorts and a white short-sleeved collared shirt. He wore tennis shoes with no socks. I immediately told Michael someone is in our yard! Not happy about getting dressed, he headed out to check things out. But after scouring the backyard, he reported that there was no one there. When I played back the security camera footage, all you could see was a streak of light tracing the path I'd seen him take across the lawn just a few minutes before.

FROM THE OTHER SIDE OF THE BED

Now this was creepy! Before my husband retired, he would leave for work at around 7:00 a.m. One morning I had gone back to sleep after he left, with my back to his side of the bed. Feeling that creepy sensation that I was being watched, I woke up and just lay there, wondering what it could be. Turning around to look towards hubby's side, I saw a man on the other side of the bed. With his feet planted on the floor and his elbows resting on the mattress, he leaned towards me with his face coming about two feet from mine. In my panic, the best I could do was to let out a severely muffled pathetic scream, and luckily even this muted version was enough to get him/it to disappear.

THE FRIEND STRIKES AGAIN?

A few weeks after returning home from my trip outlined in Chapter 12, I was sitting up in bed watching TV while making out my grocery list for the next day. My husband had already fallen asleep. Right by the side of my bed was the sound of water falling onto the floor. I looked up and then around to see where it could be coming from. I could hear it but didn't see any water! The sound kept getting louder and louder. I decided I better wake up Michael, so I reached over and tapped his arm and said, "Michael, do you hear that? I think a water pipe broke."

As Michael was waking up, something took it's hand placing it on my forehead and pushed me down on the bed, continuing to hold me down. I was paralyzed, not being able to move or scream! When Michael woke up and looked at me, he was shocked to see the indentations of fingers holding my arms down. He grabbed me and hugged me causing whatever it was to stop. Neither one of us actually saw anything. I couldn't help but wonder if it was something that followed me home or was sent from my friend's house that I stayed at in Chapter 12.

16

Afterlife
Thoughts
✝

Pam Mandel

A lot of people believe in some sort of an afterlife. The Bible is very clear in John 14:2 that Jesus goes to prepare a place for us, and not just any place, but a mansion with many rooms. The controversy is not as much whether there is an afterlife but more with whether or not ghost exists. Can a loved one after death come back into our dimension? Can that loved one who passed away interact with us? We are definitely not experts on this topic, but our experiences have shown us both that our loved ones can visit, and we believe God's grace allows them to comfort us at times.

The day our grandpa died, while feeding him dinner, he kept repeating over and over to me that grandma was here. My grandma had passed away in the early 60's. As he pointed over to the door, I turned and didn't see anything. Hours later he passed away.

Around a month before my mom died, I was walking past her bedroom door and saw her mother, my grandma, sitting at her bedside. "Hmmm, I thought, what could this be about?" I quickly had a moment back in time to who my grandpa had seen just before he passed. So, deep down I had a strong feeling and a month later our mom succumbed to her final heart attack and was gone. I thought at the time, "well if I see grandma sitting on my bed, I will know my time is near." Needless to say, I am in no hurry to see my grandma.

Two years later, during the 2020 COVID 19 pandemic, I got the flu and pneumonia in my left lung. I was so sick for almost a month, and there were several moments when it was so hard for me to breathe that I thought I was going to see her. Every time my sister would call to check on me, I would reply "I haven't seen her on the side of my bed yet, so I think I might survive this!" Fortunately, though, I never saw my grandma and survived the pneumonia.

When my grandma was in the hospital dying of cancer at the age of 60, she kept asking my mom what time it was. When my mom replied with the time, grandma would say, "It is almost time". Shortly afterwards, she passed away. I always wondered when I heard this story, how did she know? Was a love one from the other side there with her giving her the countdown to her final minute? Maybe it was her mom sitting on the edge of her hospital bed.

Our stories of our dogs passing have proven to us that there is an afterlife for them also. Occasionally, we will see them dashing across the floor. Michael and I have heard a dog collar banging against our dog's water bowl. However, our dogs are on the bed with us. I have no explanation for it except it could be one of our deceased dogs drinking.

These stories show that God's love manifested by Him, at times, sends our dead love ones to come and be with us in those final hours. We believe that all of this can aid us in the transition to the other side. The one thing we know for sure is when it is Karen and my time, our mom, grandma, and maybe great-grandma will be right there sitting on the edge of our bed.

As women of faith, it has been a complicated journey when it comes to our belief in ghosts. Our dilemma comes with the sixty-plus years of having supernatural gifts that allow us to see and feel spiritual energies in other dimensions. Although a large percentage of our experiences have been with angels and demons, there remains a substantial percentage that just can't be explained in simple terms. Sometimes ghost appear at the age that they passed away, others much younger when they were at their healthiest.

We believe time does not exist in the afterlife. That said, it's funny because we believe spirits can multi-task, being in more than one place at a time. Essentially, we believe that spirits consist of pure energy, even at times appearing as different size orbs flying in their own formations. Spirits are intelligent and can cause many events to happen. Some examples of this would include anxiety, mood swings, touching, talking, taking personal items, unexplainable noises, shutting doors, unlocking doors, and manipulating electronics. In our experiences, some of the ways they can manifest are a gray mist, a black silhouette, or a solid apparition. Although we understand the skeptic mentality, for those of you who believe in the afterlife, there is such comfort in knowing your loved ones are happy and healthy. Whether it is a person or an animal, when your grieving is over, you can finally take a deep breath and believe they have just moved into a different part of their journey in this complex universe. The good news is we will all see our loved ones again; they are not gone forever.

Many of us who have experienced the loss of loved ones have felt their love after their death. Maybe it is their smell, a loving touch, a vision, or something even a little more. After our dad's death, there was his pipe smell, seven knocks on our headboard on the 1st birthday after his death on April 7th, and a hug that was full of so much love it had to be heavenly.

For those of you who do not believe in the afterlife, you will have a wonderful surprise!

The following are true stories from relatives that have lost their love ones.

JUDY'S STORIES

My husband of forty-seven years passed away October 23, a moment I never believed would come. I functioned those first several days out of what had to be taken care of, which kept me going.

My birthday was six days after Richard's death, October 29. I got up early that morning, not caring about my birthday. I entered into the kitchen to make some coffee and turned on my wax-warming decoration in my kitchen. The apartment was dark. I looked up and on the wall were two hearts together. I had never seen that reflection before. I instantly felt Richard saying, "I love you, and I'm here on your day." That was my first visit from Richard.

"I looked up and on the wall were two hearts together..."

My second visit was four months later. I was preparing a soup to take to a Bible study group. I had a potato to chop up. I took the knife and started to cut through the potato when I heard, "Be careful, Judy. Don't cut yourself. "

Richard always would tell me that since we were first married after a cutting injury to my hand when I was slicing a tomato. I put the knife down and could feel the presence of my husband behind me as if his arms were around me. The feeling of love was so strong I had to turn around and look. I felt such love. I wept and thanked him for his presence and for the presence of God I felt. After a few moments the feeling grew weaker and he was gone. I gained such strength that day knowing Richard was always near and with me.

During the sixth month of my husband's passing, my granddaughter Emma was working on a college assignment. She was so close to her papa and missed him terribly. She deals with her sorrow quietly. Well, she looked up from her laptop and was staring out her bedroom window when all of a sudden, she felt her papa's hand on her shoulder. Emma said the world paused.

She told me, "Grandma, papa visited me!"

I told her, "I know he's with you. He's so proud of you and is watching over you with so much love."

Now I have a two-year-old granddaughter. Chloe was nine months old when we came to Las Vegas to live closer to our son after we lost our home in California to a fire. Chloe gravitated to her papa. She loved to sit with him. She was eighteen months old when her papa passed away.

I asked Chloe, "Where's papa?"

She looked up to the sky and waved. Often without asking Chloe about papa, you will see her looking up and waving. I believe this little one sees and feels her papa's love, even so young.

The spiritual world is real.

DOREEN'S STORIES

Mom passing:

My mom passed away at the age of eighty-six. During the funeral, I was sitting with my sister and daughter when all three of us saw a silhouette of my mom appear wearing a white flowing gown sitting on the side of the altar. She was in her twenties with the biggest smile on her face. All three of us saw it at the same time. We all knew my mom was letting us know she is no longer sick and very happy.

Radio:

We moved into a newer home, and while I was alone unpacking, I said out loud, "Dad, I wish you could see our new home." My dad had passed away a few months earlier. All of a sudden, I could hear music playing. Following where the music was coming from, it led me to the basement. I could tell it was coming from one of the boxes. When I started to go through them, I eventually found my dad's old Club's Radio. The radio hadn't worked for years, but right at that moment it started to play even though it was unplugged and broken. I just knew it was my dad saying, "I am here, Doreen!"

Grandfather's passing:

I was sitting on the couch with my grandfather when he looked at me and said very quietly, "Do you see the angels?" Later that night, I was at home asleep and suddenly woke up and said "Grandpa!" Just then the phone rang, and my mother answered it. My mother informed me that grandpa had just died. I was nineteen years old at the time.

Karen, Mom, and Pam in 2016

17

Going
Forward

✝

Pam Mandel

2020

My sister and I have just opened our hearts and shared with you some of our most memorable paranormal experiences. Some we have never talked about before except with each other because of the stigmatism that is associated with these occurrences.

Many times, the activity begins with just one person in

the house. At times, negative entities wait for that exact moment when you're alone, then they move in to terrorize that individual. There is no one to validate what just happened—no one to share their paranormal experience—most of the time, no one to believe them.

Listening to others share their paranormal stories and comparing those with ours, it is clear that one of the greatest goals of the entities is to make us and others believe we are losing our faculties.

Being far from experts in the paranormal field, we have dedicated our book to all the paranormal investigators, parapsychologists, historians, religious leaders, and "gifted" individuals who have worked tirelessly to alleviate the fear and anxiety in those experiencing unknown paranormal phenomenon. If you are experiencing paranormal events, there are so many programs on television, as well as excellent books, that can help you understand what you are going through. Most important, they can assure you that you are not alone, and confirm you are not crazy.

Being open to the phenomena, there is no end. Experiences continue to occur. Spirits surround each and every one of us. We never stop depending on God's love and strength as we move forward with paranormal activity still in our lives, like the ups and downs of a roller coaster ride.

The one thing we are sure of is it only takes one experience for a skeptic to become a believer!

Pam and Karen during the COVID-19 Pandemic in June 2020

CPSIA information can be obtained
at www.ICGtesting.com
Printed in the USA
LVHW022203070820
662367LV00016B/458